READING
THE 1950s

READING
THE 1950s

STUART HYLTON

The
History
Press

First published in 1997 by Sutton Publishing
This new edition published in 2013

The History Press
The Mill, Brimscombe Port
Stroud, Gloucestershire, GL5 2QG
www.thehistorypress.co.uk

British Library Cataloguing in Publication Data.
A catalogue record for this book is available from the British
Library.

ISBN 978 0 7524 9353 4

Typesetting and origination by The History Press
Printed in Great Britain

Contents

Introduction and Acknowledgements 7

1. 1950: Out of Austerity 9

2. 1951: Festival Time 19

3. 1952: The King Dies 35

4. 1953: Coronation 45

5. 1954: Teddy Boys and Tragedy 57

6. 1955: Smog and ITV 67

7. 1956: Rock Around the Clock 79

8. 1957: Space, and Room to Live 91

9. 1958: Banning the Bomb, and the Smoke 103

10. 1959: Minis and Mikardo 115

PALACE

County Theatre (Reading), Ltd.   'Phone 3440
THE PREMIER THEATRE OF BERKSHIRE
BOX OFFICE OPEN 10 a.m. to 9 p.m.

6.15   MONDAY, MARCH 1st   TWICE NIGHTLY   8.25

Pete Collins SAYS — 17TH YEAR — 10TH NEW EDITION

"WOULD YOU BELIEVE IT!"

SEE —

THE TALLEST WOMAN IN THE WORLD! 8 FEET, 4½ INCHES IN HER NYLONS!

THE MAN WHO EXPLODES A LIVE BOMB ON HIS CHEST!

THE MACHINE THAT SHAVES A MAN WITH AN ORDINARY RAZOR!

GLAMOUR ON THE GLOBE

THE HUMAN OSTRICH HE SWALLOWS A LIGHTED ELECTRIC BULB — YOU CAN SEE IT GLOW!

THE WOMAN WITH TEN BRAINS!

THE WORLD'S FATTEST FAMILY — THEY WEIGH HALF A TON!

THE LIVING FOUNTAIN A WORLD-FAMOUS HUMAN MIRACLE!

ARTHUR FORSHAW

THE STRANGEST SHOW THE WORLD HAS EVER SEEN! ★

Introduction and Acknowledgements

After I wrote my first book about Reading – *Reading Places, Reading People* – I promised myself I would never do another one on the subject. But this will be my fourth book about Reading, and I would be far less confident in predicting that there might not one day be a fifth!

My previous book, *Reading at War*, looked at how the ordinary people of Reading fared through the extraordinary events of the war years. The 1950s were in some ways even more dramatic in the changes they wrought in ordinary people's lives. The decade took us right from postwar austerity to the swinging sixties of the Beatles and the Mini. During those years we saw the introduction of many of the conveniences that we take for granted today. Television came into its own and the motor car – for better or worse – began to dominate our travel habits and many other aspects of our lives. It saw the heralding of a new Elizabethan era in Britain and the beginning of the space age worldwide.

All of these radical changes were reflected in the lives of the average citizen of Reading. At the same time, the town was wrestling with its own domestic problems – the housing shortage, the pressure on schools and public services from a growing population and the first signs of the town's change from a mainly industrial economy to one based on services.

Once again, I have used the pages and pictures of the *Berkshire Chronicle* to tell the story. All human life is reflected in them – courage and infamy; vision (both the genuine article and the confident predictions that are way off-target); and what is to us the innocence of an age that perceives such things as the launderette and the multi-storey car park as miracles of modern technology. Last, but by no means least, there is the humour – conscious and unintended – of the era. We see both the ingenuity and the incompetence of the local criminal classes; the ability of officialdom and the thundering editorial column to get it completely wrong; and the values and attitudes that remind us that 1950s Reading was vastly different from the present-day community.

My thanks as ever go to Margaret Smith and her colleagues at the Local Studies Library at Berkshire's Central Library in Reading, who hold the historic copies of the *Chronicle*. Thanks are also due to Karen Hull, Javier Pes and their colleagues in Reading Borough Council's Museum Service, which is now custodian of the *Reading Chronicle* collection of photographs for this period. The Berkshire Newspaper Company, which publishes what is now the *Reading Chronicle*, kindly gave their permission to quote from the pages of its predecessor and supported the publication of this book in other ways.

Last, but by no means least, my thanks go to my long-suffering family who, having recently relived the war years at second hand, have now endured the whole of the fifties within twelve months, without too many visible signs of ageing!

ONE

1950: Out of Austerity

Reading was still struggling with the aftermath of war as the second half of the twentieth century dawned. The damage caused by bombing in the very heart of the town centre was yet to be repaired. Power cuts brought all-too-frequent reminders of the blackout and many goods were still on ration.

Reading people marked the arrival of the 1950s in all sorts of ways. The dance halls and churches were equally full. Railwaymen saw in the New Year by sounding their locomotive whistles. In the week between Christmas and New Year, one of their passengers, a drunken reveller on the London to Penzance train, chose to step out at Reading for a spot of fresh air to clear his head. Unfortunately for him, the train did not stop at Reading and he did not survive to see the 1950s. At the other end of the mortal coil, Mrs Annie Gains of Whitley saw in the new decade by giving birth to a son in the back seat of a taxi, en route to the Grove Maternity Home in Emmer Green.

Although the nation was still living in the shadow of the war, signs of a new way of life were beginning to emerge. Helicopters, the newspapers announced, were going to be the transport of the future and they demanded to know what the town was doing to prepare for this. Rooftop landing pads were urgently needed. Car ownership was spreading, though new cars were still often difficult to obtain. In the second-hand market, £99 would buy a 1933 Morris Minor two-seater saloon, while a brand new Humber Pullman limousine (the stretched limo of its day) cost £1,350 plus purchase tax (or roughly twice the cost of a two-bedroom cottage in Caversham).

Perhaps even more significantly, a new form of home entertainment was starting to come into its own. The advertisements spoke very highly of it:

> Whatever the family choice of entertainment, you will find it in TELEVISION. It has brought a new meaning into home life and thousands who used to seek their entertainment outside, now find their television set a source of untold pleasures at home. Why not learn more about it?

Home trials were available, before you decided to make the sizeable investment of £54 or more in a set of your own. A major irritation was cars without suppressors, which affected reception. As the television-viewing public grew in number, there was hope that the fitting of suppressors to cars would be made compulsory.

Television arrives to take over our lives.

All the glamour of washday!

For those who could not afford a television, there was something else to watch – a self-service launderette.

It is the first in Berkshire and follows a pattern which has made launderettes top favourites for household washing in America and with British housewives in many towns. Standing in the garden of an eighteenth-century cottage, Reading's most original laundry is light, airy and decorated throughout in blue and white . . . . Customers bring all their family wash, from blankets to handkerchiefs, receive a cupful of special soap powder and are allotted to a machine. Mrs M. Jones, the trained attendant, shows newcomers how to pack the soiled clothes into the electric washing machine. The glass door is closed; a small dial is set and the customer sits back to watch operations. . . . even men can manage their own washing under this system, which has clear advantages in hygiene – each person's laundry is washed separately under their own supervision.

For most people, the radio and the cinema remained the main sources of entertainment. Radio stars were household names and a variety bill made up of 'Stars of Radio' appeared at the Palace Theatre in the spring of 1950. It was headed by a ventriloquist, Peter Brough (and his better-known dummy, Archie Andrews). In case anyone else finds it odd that a ventriloquist should make his name on the radio, the bill also included a troupe of dancers and a duo mysteriously described as 'Thrills on wheels', neither of which sound like an obvious act for that medium. It seems only the radio juggler was missing.

At the cinema, the Central and Granby cinemas experimented with midnight matinées, and many people queued in the rain to see *Little Women* or the Alfred Hitchcock film *Under Capricorn*. The bus company laid on special late-night buses for the filmgoers. They bought a combined cinema and bus ticket on the way in and, while they watched the film, the bus company worked out how many buses would be needed afterwards and called them up. The British film, *The Blue Lamp*, which gave birth to the character of Dixon of Dock Green, was attracting a great deal of interest in 1950. A special showing was organised at the Odeon for the Chief Constable and many of his staff. Chief Constable Lawrence said afterwards, 'It is an extremely important film, from the official police point-of-view.'

The first postwar Labour Government was coming towards its end and the hostility between Reading's Labour MP, Ian Mikardo, and the local press was growing more fierce by the week. This editorial from January 1950 is typical:

> The Socialist party knows that, in the coming General Election, whatever the hoardings may flaunt, they are on trial, and have to face a barrage of unpleasant facts which, over the past five years, have proved how much easier it is to promise than to perform. In 1945 they were suddenly and unexpectedly called upon to translate into reality the blueprints of the dreamers and the pseudo-philosophers who, for half a century, had asked only to be allowed to put their theories to the test. And what a dismal failure this translation has been! Instead of devoting their energies to restoring the war-wracked nation to at least some of its former prosperity, the Government at once plunged into the task of implementing their ideals in the face of every economic warning from more sober and expert guides; proceeded to placate by class legislation those who had put them into power; and to pass over the real government of the country into other hands.

Mikardo, for his part, took the paper to task for sending their fashion, rather than their political, correspondent to one of his speeches, since he spent all his time reporting what Mikardo was wearing and nothing about what he had said – and even managed to get the details of his attire wrong! Maybe it was this that led the paper to involve its ultimate weapon – the Women's Page – in the election. They sent their reporter to spend an afternoon canvassing with the wife of one of the candidates (the Conservative, naturally).

As the elections approached, the paper campaigned furiously for a change of MP. For this election, Reading had been split into two seats and Mikardo was standing for Reading South. In their pen portraits of the rival candidates, the paper made not the slightest pretence at impartiality. Of Mikardo, they said, 'No other candidate arouses more feeling among friend or foe' and, referring to his previous career in the private sector, suggested that 'It is typical of Mikardo that, while he condemns capitalism and free enterprise, he is quite prepared to make a good living helping capitalism and free enterprise.' By contrast, his Conservative opponent, David Rissik, was portrayed in near-saintly terms. He was a war hero who 'didn't just fight in the jungle; he knew what he was fighting for'.

The campaign drew a variety of well-known speakers to the town. Herbert Morrison put the Labour case at a public meeting, while Quentin Hogg came to Reading for the Conservatives and threatened to slap a writ on a man who was heckling him! The Liberals were also campaigning, though one gets the impression that their hearts were not really in it. They were being criticised in the press for splitting the anti-Labour vote and their electoral slogan 'For a liberal government vote Liberal' did not immediately seize the public imagination for some reason. Their candidate for Reading North, Michael Derrick, addressed what was not surprisingly described as 'a small audience' at Kendrick School on the uplifting theme of 'If we fail, we shall try again'. Small wonder, perhaps, that they only got just over 3,000 votes in each of the Reading constituencies.

The country returned the Labour government for a second term, but with the slimmest of majorities, and Reading elected two Labour MPs, Mikardo and Kim Mackay ('a disastrous choice' the paper called it). Characteristically, Mikardo could not resist a piece of sarcasm at the *Chronicle*'s expense in the light of his victory:

> I am thankful for the service they have rendered to the Labour cause during the election campaign. People are not dumb and they are not taken in by such vituperation and, far from supporting the cause they are urged to, they oppose it. There were hundreds of 'floating voters' who voted for us on the basis of what the senile old gentleman who writes the leaders for the *Berkshire Chronicle* said. I do sincerely want to thank him for putting some doubtful voters into our camp which we should not otherwise have had.

When, later that year, Mikardo was rushed to hospital with a gall bladder problem, the editorial columns were strangely silent in their wishes for a speedy recovery.

One of the commonest criticisms of the government was that it was imposing its ideology on aspects of life where it was not needed. There were editorial calls for housing to be removed from the realm of party politics (that is, Labour party politics) so that free enterprise could rapidly reduce waiting lists, and the prospective Conservative candidate for Reading South made the following attack at a local by-election meeting:

> National policies have been forced into local government. That has been the work of the Socialists. In our view, local government must be 100% local, and one of our first objectives when we are returned will be to see that our local councils get back the powers that have been stripped from them.

Local councils in the 1990s are still waiting for a government of any persuasion that will do this.

Housing remained a major problem for many people in Reading. In July 1950 the 1,000th postwar house was handed over to its new tenants at Halls Road in Tilehurst. Mr and Mrs Slater, the happy occupants, had been waiting five years for it and there were still more than 4,000 families like them on the town's waiting lists. Many solutions (other than private enterprise) were offered to the housing problem. Some saw industrialised building methods as the answer and 128 concrete houses were built in Whitley at a cost of £158,544 5s 8d. These, the public were told, kept the costs down without spoiling the beauty of the surrounding area (in this case, Whitley Wood Road). Wokingham Rural District Council believed terraced houses were one possible answer. As one of the councillors noted, during a fact-finding mission to look at this form of building:

> They can be things of beauty and frightfully economical as well. In the past, we have made the mistake of putting people into houses they cannot afford. We do not want any more of this nonsense of two lavatories, one upstairs and one downstairs. I hope this council is going to turn its back on semi-detached houses with rents of 30s a week.

The courts continued to offer up their selection of life's rich tapestry. A man was arrested under a 600-year-old piece of legislation for masquerading as a woman at the Rex cinema 'in a manner likely to cause a breach of the peace' (presumably as opposed to masquerading as a woman in any other way). No details were given to an eager public, except that he was bound over to keep the peace in the sum of £100. In another case, an 81-year-old man who had spent a total of fifty-six years in prison had another four added to his total, for a case of housebreaking.

The motoring offences at one quarter sessions were of more than usual interest, as the defendant in a case of driving without due care and attention was a 20-year-old racing motorist named Stirling Moss. It was alleged that he took a corner at excess speed, with his tyres squealing. At his appeal, his defence counsel described the £10 fine, the endorsement of his licence and a month's suspension as 'a slur on a racing motorist', but the appeal was unsuccessful. (We will never know whether the arresting officer was the first to ask the immortal question 'And who do you think you are, then, Stirling Moss?')

One of the oddest cases of the year involved a motorist charged with two counts of dangerous driving. Despite narrowly missing a man in an invalid chair, hitting a car and a motor-cycle and turning his car on its side, his plea that he was suffering from the effects of sunstroke at the time was enough to get him acquitted.

One important question settled by the courts was the value of a wife. A man from Ringwood Road made a claim for £50 against the co-respondent in his divorce case for the loss of his wife. The learned judge's summing up included the following remarks:

> It is all too common for a co-respondent who has broken up a man's home to
> evade the consequences of his wrongdoing by what some people might call a
> mean trick, saying 'The woman I took away from you was not worth very much
> anyway, and you are not entitled to anything for having lost her.'

The judge took the view that £50 damages was very reasonable, and threw in
the custody of their child for good measure.

Two men engaged in a potentially hazardous form of theft, appearing
before the courts for stealing a quantity of lead from the Atomic Energy
Establishment at Harwell. Anyone seeking to copy their crime in future would
have less travelling to do, as it was announced early in 1950 that Reading
was to get its own Atomic Energy Establishment, on the former wartime
bomber airfield at Aldermaston. The government took pains to ensure the
public that 'precautions will be taken to ensure that no harmful effect to
the neighbourhood will arise from the works to be carried out at this new
establishment'. Then as now, the authorities were not forthcoming when
asked to be more specific about security.

Opinion was sharply divided between those who wanted to keep the
picturesque village as it was and those who saw jobs and business opportunities.
Plans were subsequently announced to build 500 homes to house the workers
at the Establishment, in Newbury and Basingstoke, as well as in Aldermaston
itself. The authorities in Reading were afraid that all this building would
draw essential labour away from the house- and school-building programmes
in Reading itself – both The Hill and Geoffrey Field Schools were getting
seriously behind schedule. The council set up a group to monitor the effects of
construction work at Aldermaston. Their fears proved to be well-founded. By
1951 the lure of free transport to Harwell and Aldermaston and payment for
the time spent travelling proved too much for many people working in Reading,
and the council had over a hundred vacancies for building tradesmen.

The *Chronicle* seemed to align itself with the modernisers:

> One only has to think of the power grids that cross the land, the perfection of the
> internal combustion engine, of radio and radar, and the miracle of speed in the
> air, to realise that no part of the countryside is now remote or free from incursion
> and no rural settlement able to concern itself only with its traditional activities.

The bureaucracy that had burgeoned in the war years showed few signs of
abating. There were complaints that the housing programme was being held
back by the need to get government approval for every tender. A Mr Talfourd-
Cook had more direct experience of government bureaucracy in action. Having
taken his suits to the cleaners, when he returned to collect them, he found that
government-appointed bailiffs had taken over the shop as a result of the owner's
tax arrears. They refused to hand over his suits, even in return for payment of
the cleaning bills, and he subsequently had to buy his own clothes back at a sale
of goods, at a cost of £13 15s. Mr Talfourd-Cook took the matter up directly
with the Chancellor of the Exchequer, and eventually received a refund and a
letter of apology from Stafford Cripps.

Nationalisation had been one of the big issues for the election and the papers carried extensive advertising, singing the praises of a private-sector steel industry. The paper itself (an opponent of nationalisation) missed no opportunity to attack state-run enterprises. Even a report that the Gas Board offices in Friar Street were having electric light installed led them to attack state control for doing away with competition. If the editor was trying to be ironic, the joke was not obvious even all these years later.

Even with the election won, Ian Mikardo showed that he had lost none of his powers to fuel controversy. In an article in *Tribune*, he suggested that people who lived in areas like Amity Road and voted Conservative were snobs, who felt they really belonged in Caversham Heights. This caused a huge outcry among working-class Conservative voters in Reading (aided not a little by the local press). Mikardo's response was to go down to Amity Road with a loudspeaker van and address the locals. Numbers of them took him (rather firmly, no doubt) into their homes, to prove that they were not the slum-dwellers that he had described in his article.

Also active in 1950 was God. The Vicar of Christ Church, the Revd E.H. Knell, announced plans for an evangelistic campaign on the Whitley Estate. He described it in military terms as 'an attack' and added 'it is a formidable task but one that has to be faced'. A more apocalyptic view was taken by the Revd Oswald C. Goold, who announced that his work at St Mary's, Castle Street, was coming to an end:

The steel industry fought a rearguard action against the government's nationalisation plans.

I believe that, to the intelligent Christian, the dreadful times in which we are living point to the fact that the great Head of the Church is coming soon, and that you and I are living in the last days of this dispensation. My one concern is that, when I lay down my charge and meet Him, I shall have His 'Well done'.

Encouraging signs that rationing was gradually being phased out began to appear during the course of 1950. Points values on various goods were reduced. This led to a tremendous rush for sweet things that forced some retailers to introduce their own impromptu forms of rationing. Petrol came off rationing just before the Whitsun bank holiday and beer was returning to its prewar strength. As if this were not joy enough, families were even allowed one point-free packet of that wartime 'favourite', powdered egg. New forms of convenience food were also starting to make their appearance.

At this time Birds Eye 'frosted' green beans and Batchelor's chicken noodle soup in a packet were both available and the advertsisements for them came complete with instructions for cooking these exotic new products. Eighty old people in Reading got an early chance to try the delights of frozen food. The Reading Philanthropic Institution delivered frozen Christmas dinners to them on Christmas Eve, complete with instructions for heating them up the next day.

However, soap was still rationed until September. In July, a newsprint shortage resulted in the local paper being reduced to its wartime size for a time, much to their editorial dismay, and the launch of a paper salvage campaign had strong wartime overtones. The Ladies' Page of the wartime newspaper had become the Women's Page and, among the diet of fashion and home-centred items, there was the start of a recognition that women might have careers:

Reading wives learn about the miracle of frozen food.

The American Department of Labour recently conducted a survey in the department stores, banks, insurance offices and industrial plants of four major American cities to find out why women seldom held the top jobs. Lack of confidence in the women themselves, 'company policy' and the attitude that high level management posts should be held by men are some of the reasons given in the survey, which revealed that women who had achieved good positions in the spheres mentioned were not predominantly university educated. In many cases, long experience appeared to count for more.

The survey showed that over half of bank employees in the sample were women, compared with 40 per cent in 1939, yet none of the bank presidents were women. The Women's Page asked:

> What have Reading business women to say about the positions they now hold, compared with the chances of promotion ten years ago? Do any of them feel that their sex prevents them from reaching top positions?

The answer from the correspondence columns of the following editions was a deafening silence.

The royal family still retained a prominent place in the affections of the public, as this editorial, written on the occasion of the birth of Princess Anne, shows:

> Despite the troubles that beset it, Britain is a fortunate land in which loyalty to the Monarchy and affection for the King and Queen and their family are so happily conjoined. Since their wedding three years ago, the Princess and her husband have found their way into the hearts of the people by their unassuming charm and regard for their high duties.

Also dear to the hearts of local people was Reading Football Club, even though the team finished tenth in the Third Division – its lowest postwar position. The club made a loss of £957 17s 7d on the 1949/50 season, no doubt aided by the lavish £6,000 it spent in the transfer market in the course of the year. The review of the season bemoaned their low gates – though 25,000 supporters turned up to see the team knocked out of the FA Cup in the third round by Doncaster, and even a pre-season practice game drew a crowd of nearly 8,000. In those days, the club ran four teams and had a total of 32 professional players on its books.

As postwar traffic grew, there were moves to introduce better traffic management. However, the term meant something very different in 1950. There were calls for the pedestrian crossings on the Friar Street/West Street junction to be removed, because they impeded the free flow of traffic, and plans for easing the traffic problems of Broad Street included not pedestrianisation but railings to keep the walking public back out of the way of the motorist.

The news that Berkshire was to get its own 'satellite town' at Bracknell got the editorial column thinking about the amenities it would need:

> When the new satellite towns take shape there will presumably be planned 'pubs'. One of the tasks of the planner should be to incorporate in the new houses of refreshment the warmth, colour and welcome of the old English inn. There is an intangible atmosphere about an ancient hostelry, for time lays its hand on everything man contrives and gives it a touch of pleasing decay. Uneven roofline and irregular chimneys; smoke-stained rafters; worn red quarries on the taproom floor; huge open fireplaces with glowing logs; all are eloquent features that have an appeal to many besides the bucolic; and few of those old varnished sporting prints and glass-cased pike and perch would hang comfortably upon the plumb ruler surface of synthetic coloured walls.

After waxing equally lyrical about settles and shove-halfpenny boards, it concluded: 'Perhaps the planners should have all these desiderata in mind; but they should be warned that the country inn has a long pedigree and is held in great affection by those who use it.'

Apart from the planners, the greatest threat to civilisation was seen to come from our former wartime allies in Russia. A thousand volunteer civil defence workers were sought to help protect the people of Reading from the effects of atomic war. Among the instructions available from them were some on reinforcing your wartime Anderson shelter to cope with nuclear weapons. The volunteers included a couple of people in their eighties who, as seventy-something youngsters, had done their bit for civil defence in the Second World War.

Winter brought with it the fogs that disrupted normal life and threatened the health of many. One in December lasted from Friday night to Monday afternoon. Fog was graded according to severity – category B was where visibility was reduced to 55 yards. One just before Christmas was so dense that it brought traffic to a virtual standstill.

As Christmas approached, at least there were none of the wartime shortages of items to buy as presents. Among the things people had managed without for years were a Corona fruit squash decanter, complete with presentation box, for 3s 9d and a three-dimensional Dresda Ware wall plaque which, the advertisement assured us, was quite 'the present vogue in home decoration' (prices from 17s 6d).

Children in 1950 could be forgiven for getting confused about Father Christmas. Depending on which advertisement you believed, he was either landing in an aeroplane on Kings Meadow and being carried in a space ship (one wonders why he bothered with anything as old hat as an aeroplane) to a moon rocket grotto in McIlroys, accompanied by a host of fairy folk; arriving with his band and Cinderella, to spend the pre-Christmas period in the Cinderella grotto at Heelas; travelling in the speedboat SS *Reading* to the Co-op; or accompanying Saba, Snowball and Mr Walrus to the frozen north of Wellsteeds.

The police appealed for people to use the car parks in the run-up to Christmas, rather than trying to park on-street. No doubt the streets themselves were filled with the rival Santas' sleighs, speedboats and spaceships.

TWO

1951: Festival Time

The year began with Reading carpeted with snow. Despite the fact that it apparently lay only four inches deep, it succeeded in plunging the town into chaos. There were car crashes everywhere, 2,200 phone lines were down in the Reading area and there were widespread power cuts. The council mobilised 'Operation Snow', calling out snow ploughs, mechanical loaders, forty extra lorries and 160 extra men, recruited from local builders and the relatively small ranks of the local unemployed.

The weather also had an adverse effect on the health of the local population. The paper reported that 'Reading is experiencing an acute shortage of men's handkerchiefs in the shops and the chemists' stores are exceptionally busy supplying 'flu and cold remedies.' One in five postmen were off with the 'flu; 10 per cent of bus staff were ill and the phone services were affected by staff shortages.

In 1851 the Victorians had held a Great Exhibition to celebrate the achievements of the most powerful nation in the world. A century later, Britain had relinquished the title of top nation, but another festival was seen as just the thing to cheer up an impoverished people. In addition to the national events, provincial communities were invited to share in the celebrations. Conservative-controlled Reading was one of the few authorities which declined to meet the cost of being affiliated to the festival. Earlier attempts to get them to contribute £800 towards the cost of the celebrations had been unsuccessful and they restricted themselves to making space in the town hall available at no cost to suitable festival events. They were supported in this by the local paper, who saw the whole thing as more Socialist profligacy, especially when nationally the festival overshot its budget by £1 million:

> The Festival of Britain has made heavy going since its inception; it has had to battle against provincial as well as national lukewarmness; it might be said to be in the category of the unwanted child. It has become a fetish with foreigners that the English take their pleasures sadly; this was never wholly true; the explanation is that on the other side of the channel the approach to fun and gaiety is differently conceived. But the Festival may serve to nourish the generalisation.

These criticisms, and others like them from Conservatives, prompted MP Ian Mikardo to attack their 'sickening hypocrisy'. He claimed that although they

Boys' Brigade runners pause from delivering their loyal message to the king for the Festival of Britain.

condemned the festival at the outset, as its popularity became evident, they would not only espouse it but would claim it to have been their own idea in the first place. There was no lack of enthusiasm for the festival on the part of the general public, judging by the number of ideas for events they put forward.

It opened with an exhibition of books in the library, a football match played at Elm Park between the youth leagues of Reading and Swindon and a festival bonfire and community singing in Hills Meadow. Despite the availability of the telephone, the Boys' Brigade chose to deliver a loyal message to the king from their members in every corner of the land by means of a series of relay runners. The king subsequently read the message in a special radio broadcast. Other ideas put forward included an industrial and retail trades exhibition in Hills Meadow, church rallies, Reading Football Club playing representative sides from Luxembourg and Switzerland, a water carnival, a public speaking competition, a painting exhibition, a youth week, a drama festival, a flower festival – in which every household put a floral display in their front window and everyone wore a buttonhole – and a historical pageant.

The paper reported that some communities were taking a very prosaic view of the festivities: 'In one village in Derbyshire, the contribution will include the provision of a public convenience, and sewerage schemes and anti-pollution stations are other alluring adjuncts to the merriment.'

Crowds around the remains of the Festival of Britain bonfire at Hills Meadow.

One other idea that caused raised eyebrows in the council, when they were asked for free space at the town hall, was a festival of television. This was seen, probably quite rightly, as a thinly disguised form of advertising, and the question was asked whether the next proposals would be festivals of record players, radios and other domestic appliances. The fact that television ownership was still far from universal was illustrated by the fact that the cinemas opened specially on the morning after the national launch of the festival, to enable the people of Reading to see the royal pageantry, with the king on the steps of St Paul's Cathedral.

Advertisers were quick to latch on to the festival theme. There were festival furniture sales, people were encouraged to buy televisions to watch the national festivities and Wrights London Macaroons rather ambitiously promised to make every meal a festival. A Reading wallpaper manufacturer even produced some special edition wallpapers for the Festival. One example was called 'Early Bird'. Designed by J.B. Priestley's daughter Sylvia, it was described as having a blackbird medallion motif on a background of lime green, white and mushroom stripes. These exclusive papers retailed for between 25s and 30s a roll – which seems a high price to pay for feeling permanently seasick in your own sitting room.

As the festival came to an end, there was a feeling that Reading's contribution to it had not been impressive:

There seems a consensus of opinion that Reading's share of the Festival of Britain
has been a very poor one. As the capital of the Royal County, it has not risen to
the occasion, nor taken advantage of its wealth of historic incident and industrial
eminence to stage a commanding contribution. . . . What is the reason for this
lethargy? From its inception the Town Council refused to shoulder any financial
responsibility for the enterprise; their late contribution was limited to the free letting
of the Town Hall and baskets of flowers on the lamp standards and trolley poles
. . . . Mr Morrison's child did not set the Thames at Reading alight; perhaps the
electors generally have had a little too much of Mr Morrison in the last few years.

Live entertainment still played an important part in people's leisure, and
amateur dramatics in particular flourished at this time. The Earley Players put
on a special production of *School for Scandal* for the festival. It is to be hoped
that their production was better received than that by the Mapledurham
Residents' Association Dramatic Section. Their performance of Wilfred
Massey's play *The Feminine Touch* appears to have been the theatrical
occasion from hell. The paper's theatre correspondent, who could normally
be relied upon to take a charitable view of the most execrable productions,
reported that the production 'had periods in which the action lumbered along
like a carthorse on the farm on which it was set; occasionally the cast lost their
grip completely and there were many demands on the prompter. There was
good material floundering for the lack of a producer with experience.' Of the
actors, the man playing farmer Edwin Markham he said 'could have been very
good indeed with toning down. He over-accented and yet his big moment in
the last scene was a flop.' The actresses fared no better. The one cast as Joanna
Cooper 'would have benefitted much from experienced advice' (such as 'take
up a different hobby'?) while the person playing Paddy Richards 'was miscast
and did not entirely believe her lines'. The most basic techniques appeared to
elude them: 'The lovers' kisses (oh Mr Producer!) were dreadful!' and even
the scenery did not escape criticism: 'the setting . . . did not quite fit with pig
feeding and cow dung'.

While understandably none of the members of this production went on to
become household names, the local variety bills were providing a good proving
ground for some who did achieve wider fame. Ventriloquist Terry Hall, before
making his name with Lenny the Lion, appeared in Reading with an Irish dummy
named Mickey Flynn. Felix Bowness, later to feature on television as the jockey
Fred Quilley in *Hi-de-hi!*, appeared on a variety programme with Vera Lynn,
where he was billed as 'that irrepressible young man'. And when the variety radio
programme *Workers' Playtime* was recorded at the Huntley & Palmers' works
canteen, the lower reaches of the bill included a young man described as 'the man
with a thousand voices'. His name was Peter Sellars. At an amateur level, the local
branch of the British Railways Staff Association held its own 21st Annual Festival
of Music and Drama. One of the most popular classes was one called 'logical
grumbling', in which competitors had to complain on a subject of their own
choosing for five minutes – nothing of a political or religious nature was allowed,
though the rail service itself does not appear to have been subject to a similar ban
on criticism.

There was certainly plenty to complain about on the railways, given that services were having to be withdrawn owing to shortages of both coal and manpower. The problem was apparently that, with full employment, many railwaymen were being lured away into labouring jobs paying 30s or £2 more. At least, so claimed Mr Harold Price, the prospective Conservative candidate for Reading South. Perhaps surprisingly, he had taken up the railwaymen's cause. The result of the inequality in wages was, more predictably, a rail strike that seriously disrupted Western Region services.

Full employment was having effects in many walks of life. A nursing shortage closed 89 of the 1,118 beds in the Reading Hospital area. The local Medical Officer of Health warned that it might be necessary to go back to the old-fashioned infirmary-style wards for the chronically sick and elderly in hospital. The council was short of men to go round and re-set the street lamps – the power cuts used to play havoc with their automatic timers, so that the lamps came on in the day and went off at night. One power cut – the result of an unexpected cold snap in May – had much wider repercussions. It put the trolley buses out of service and disabled everything from poultry incubators to women having their hair permed.

In the previous chapter we heard about the judge who valued a wife at £50. In another court case at the Berkshire Assizes a few months later, the aggrieved husband would have set the price much lower. His wife had ended an argument with him by throwing an electric fire into his bath. When, by some miracle, this failed to kill him and he recovered consciousness, she tried to strangle him. Finally she set about him with the poker, forcing him to jump naked from the upper floor window of his house and seek refuge with his neighbours. As the prosecuting counsel explained, rather superfluously, 'in the past few years the couple have not got on very well'. She was cleared of attempted murder, but got four years for grievous bodily harm with intent.

Domestic discord was not limited to husbands and wives. One man found himself up before the Reading magistrates for assaulting his father-in-law. Cyril Petty and his victim had both already been bound over to keep the peace when, early one morning, Cyril broke down the parental bedroom door, pulled back the bedclothes and administered a sound thrashing with a piece of gas tubing. He was quite unrepentant about it when he appeared in court. 'If I had a dog whip, I would have used it. My intention was to hit him in the good old-fashioned place but he wriggled about.'

In what must have been one of the oddest crimes of the year, residents of a house in Tilehurst surprised an intruder who was in the course of stealing a wallet containing £3. The intruder surprised the residents rather more, by the fact that he was wearing nothing but a pair of boxing gloves. While they were still screaming, he made his escape into some nearby woods. Another ingenious criminal stole a lawn-mower from one house, pushed it to another and offered to cut their lawn for payment. Once he received his payment, he departed, leaving the mower behind. The police were left looking for the thief *and* the owner of the mower.

Helping yourself from people's houses may have been illegal, but it was the growing fashion in Reading's shopping streets, as this item from the Women's Page showed:

Self-service began to spread through Reading town centre.

SELF-SERVICE SHOPPING POPULAR

Are Reading's shopping habits changing? Recent months have seen the changeover of half a dozen of the town's stores to self-service methods and the latest development is the opening of a self-service tea bar. Almost without exception, the new style of shopping has pleased both customers and store keepers and there has been remarkably little reluctance to accept the experiment.

The basis of the new method is 'visual appeal' – a sound piece of 'sales psychology' now applied to every phase of advertising and selling. If a woman sees an article she is more likely to buy it than if she has to ask for it. Self-service means that the housewife walks into a spacious shop, takes a basket and wanders past tiers of goods uniformly displayed, with everything clearly marked. She finds the things she originally wanted and is given a reminder of others as her eye is caught. Finally, an assistant checks her purchases and she transfers them to her own basket.

One local shopkeeper reports a threefold increase in turnover and felt that the new method would become universal, since salesmanship was a dying art among retail staff. Another advantage is a definite decrease in shoplifting and it saves time waiting to be served.

One business that was not doing so well was the People's Pantry. The restaurant had reopened after its disastrous bombing in 1943, but had lost money in three successive years. Despite claims that it performed a valuable service for those on lower incomes, the council decided to close it in 1951.

To judge from the editorial coverage of educational matters, you might be forgiven for thinking that schooling was as much an invention of socialism as nationalisation. Take this example, criticising increases in the council's budget:

The fearsome man-eater is, of course, education, which bulldozes its way
regardless of other communal needs and gets its inspiration from irresponsible
enthusiasts. He would be a puny pedant indeed who could not each year be relied
upon to think up something lacking in the cause of learning.

Even the school meals service came in for criticism, the paper claiming that
it 'has grown to such vast proportions that it threatens to affect the ordinary
rhythm of school life'. It seems that a conference of the National Association
of Head Teachers had complained about the disruption caused by the
collection of dinner money and the general waste of school and staff time; the
use of school halls and classrooms as dining halls and kitchens; the lunchtime
supervision and the smell of cooking 'eternal boiled cabbage'. There was
even a concern that school dinners were insidiously undermining the fabric
of family life, by eroding the responsibility of parents. One delegate warned
that, as a result of school dinners, 'this generation will suffer very severely
because the influence of home life is not there'. Boiled cabbage clearly had a
lot to answer for.

The editor looked back fondly to the days before the war, when the School
Medical Officer issued those children who needed it with a certificate of
malnutrition and they were fed under the old, permissive legislation. Now, he
complained, the school meals service cost the nation some £26 million a year,
despite full employment and the availability of cheap or free milk. One school
had its own way of reducing the cost of school meals (readers of a sensitive
disposition should skip the next two paragraphs):

> Georgie, one of the three chubby pigs kept since last September by pupils at Three
> Mile Cross County Modern School, was cured for bacon by the domestic science
> class on Wednesday, under the watchful eye of parents and the Women's Institute.
>
> The instructress, Miss B. Wright, supervised, but all the work was done by the
> fourteen-year-old girls who have helped to rear the pigs. . . . The pig was killed
> in front of the children, who apparently regarded its death as a natural event and
> showed no obvious emotion. . . . on Wednesday the whole school lunched on the
> odd pieces of Georgie's well-covered body.

One real problem that was affecting schools was the shortage of space. The
move to increase the school-leaving age to fifteen had not taken account of
the effect this would have on accommodation needs. Severe overcrowding was
the result and there were even suggestions that the school-leaving age should
be temporarily reduced to fourteen again, until the building programme
caught up.

Vandalism is not just a modern phenomenon. In 1951 the members of the
Local Road Safety Committee were so worried that the courtesy campaign
signs being erected on the lamp-posts would be wrecked, that they asked the
public to report any act of hooliganism they witnessed against the boards to
the police. Meanwhile, the organisers of the South Reading Community Centre
were complaining of the 'monkey-type people' who climbed on to their roof and
generally did their best to disrupt any meeting that was held there.

This was presumably a more entertaining form of recreation than staying at home to listen to a radio programme called *Younger Generation*. This involved an audience of young people putting questions to a panel which included such youth cult figures as Professor Jimmy Edwards. In what was apparently a ground-breaking piece of outside broadcasting, one edition of this programme was broadcast from the Teen-Can-Teen (a youth club on Cross Street that shared the premises of the People's Pantry). Among the questions on the minds of Reading teenagers in 1951 were 'Have barrow boys a useful place in the community?' (this from a barrow boy) and 'How can we believe all we read in the newspapers when all the reports conflict?'

One man had the answer to all the hooliganism. Lord Northesk, opening the local Festival of Britain Hobbies Exhibition by operating a model cabin cruiser by radio control, confessed to being a life-long model railway buff. In his opening speech, he said:

> We hear too much today about juvenile delinquency, and I am sure a lot of this can be traced to the fact that a lot of young people do not know what to do with their leisure and Satan finds some mischief for idle hands to do.

While on the subject of dangerous people at large in the community, the planners produced a development plan for Berkshire that looked ahead to the far-distant future of 1971. The paper's editorial coverage did not go too far into what it actually said, possibly because they did not understand it:

> It is a bulky, detailed and somewhat terrifying document to the layman and not without riddles to the expert. It is the result of considerable thought and labour on the part of those who have been charged with its preparation.

Even in 1951, the main concern with the plan was that east Berkshire in particular was:

> . . . subject to an increasing urbanising influence which has already modified its traditional character. The tentacles of that vast and unwieldy octopus known as the metropolis have now for some years been reaching out over its fair fields and gracious pastures and, unless care be taken, it will become a hotch-potch of industrial and agrarian development without settled form and individuality.

More to the point, the paper was deeply suspicious of the principle of planning anything:

> In the larger orbit, planning is tinged with rash experimentalism of a socialist character; costly to the taxpayer and futile to the national interests. . . . the economic conformation of the county is the result of some two thousand years of progressive growth, undisturbed, in the main, by bureaucratic interference. . . . whether a tithe of [the plan's] recommendations will ever be implemented within the period envisaged is extremely doubtful. It is a plan for better days.

Concerns about the urbanisation of Berkshire would have found support from John Betjeman, described in those days as 'the writer and broadcaster', rather than a poet. He gave a talk at a local meeting of the Council for the Preservation of Rural England on the subject of 'The importance of being an interfering crank'. It was claimed that Berkshire was becoming a dumping ground, what with two Atomic Weapons Establishments (Harwell was in Berkshire in those days) and the threat of a bombing range.

On the roads, those inconsiderate pedestrians were still impeding the free flow of traffic. Plans were made to remove a number of superfluous pedestrian crossings in the town (and many of the remainder were to be painted with an ingenious system of black and white stripes, following the selection of Reading as the place to conduct a trial of this nationwide scheme). The curbing of the pedestrian had the paper's full blessing:

> One of the most important matters concerning the highways is to keep the traffic moving . . . mobility is vital in this hurrying age . . . it is equally obvious that the greater the number of crossings, the greater the congestion and delay. This is particularly noticeable in Broad Street, Reading, on a busy morning. Each new advance in quickening the life of the community . . . brings with it a parallel restriction of right and privilege. Those who find it necessary to cross the highways of busy towns must bow to the inevitable; spare a little more time to reach safe venues, and avoid hesitancy. It is better not to join the cavalcade who always seem to be fearing that they will be late for their accident.

Another of the causes of traffic congestion was the amount of on-street parking. As with so many things in those days, America had the answer (at least, it did in the view of the editorial column):

> Some time ago, attention was called to the fact that in the United States the problem, there even more troublesome, is approached in a different way. A large building is erected and on its many floors cars are parked in such a way that any one vehicle can be decanted in a matter of minutes. Opposite the Reading town hall is the bombed arcade site. Is it possible for the Corporation to take time by the forelock, acquire and utilise this site in the same way as the Americans? This project is far from visionary and might at least be examined. It would pay for itself and would allow the authorities to take a firmer line in regard to those who fail to conform to reasonable parking restrictions.

A more unusual approach to parking led to one motorist appearing before the magistrates. His car was drawn up at the roadside and he was lying in a ditch beside it, with his hat over his face. A nearly-empty bottle of port lay on the seat of the car. Despite admitting that he had also been drinking quantities of Guinness and gin that day, Mr Victor Gillow firmly denied that he was unconscious through drink – he simply could not fully remember what had happened. The magistrates found this difficult to swallow, and fined him for being drunk in charge of a motor car.

In another creative piece of traffic management, Queen Victoria's statue outside the town hall was to become the focal point of a roundabout, and was to be tastefully lit by red emergency lights during power cuts. Queen Victoria reputedly did not like Reading at the best of times. She would certainly not have been amused at being illuminated like a house of ill repute.

One further innovation in transport also led to controversy. Reading's long-standing boatbuilders (and hirers), Freebody's & Cawston's, were up in arms at a decision by the council to licence the hiring of pedalos further along the Caversham Promenade. Frightfully vulgar.

A long-standing Reading employer celebrated its centenary in 1951. Serpell's Biscuits moved from Plymouth (where they were founded in 1851) to Reading in 1899. Shortly afterwards, in 1904, their factory in South Street had been destroyed by fire, but they had survived and flourished in the town.

The biggest fire of 1951 took place in nearby Mill Lane, when the premises of Philips & Son, rag merchants, were destroyed. Neighbours had to be evacuated,

The ruins of Philips & Sons' Mill Lane premises after the fire.

as eighty firefighters tackled flames 60 feet high and spectacular balls of flaming cotton wool floating into the sky. The disruption to business was less than it might have been, since the firm was already in the process of moving to new premises in Basingstoke Road.

Ian Mikardo's career as a controversialist hit new records of productivity. In a single week, he managed to get fellow MP Robert Boothby to complain to the Press Council about remarks Mikardo made on *Any Questions?* about Boothby's Commons attendance record *and* was forced to apologise in Parliament for calling a fellow Member a liar. His first attempt to modify his unparliamentary language – by describing his opponent's words as 'the opposite of the truth' – was not accepted by the Speaker. Mikardo also managed to find himself at odds with his own party on a variety of policy issues, including pensions (Mikardo wanted them paid to men aged 65+ and women aged 60+ who were medically unable to continue working).

Rearmament proceeded apace in 1951, along with the promotion of Civil Defence. Dr K. Mendelssohn of Oxford University spoke at the Reading branch of the Institution of Production Engineers on the subject of atomic energy. He thought atomic-powered vehicles would be highly unlikely, in view of the dangers of radiation and the impossibility of vehicles being able to carry sufficient protective concrete. He offered these bleak thoughts on the prospects for civil defence in Reading:

> There would be no protection against an atomic bomb dropped on Reading, except that such a bomb was expensive and Reading might not be considered a sufficiently worthwhile target.

None of this deterred the authorities' efforts to recruit over a thousand volunteers to provide civil defence in the event of a nuclear attack. The results were not altogether encouraging, and by 1951 they had only got about a third of that number. None the less, those they recruited were fully trained in the preparation of emergency meals by the School Meals service, holding out the delightful prospect of nuclear devastation *and* boiled cabbage.

One of the highlights of Reading Football Club's season was a friendly against Manchester United. Matt Busby had played for Reading throughout the war and had promised to bring his star-studded team to Elm Park. The two teams enjoyed a game of golf together beforehand at Calcot and the match itself ended in a 4–4 draw. At one point in the match, Carey, United's captain, corrected the referee's award of a goal kick to his team. Carey told him that he had kicked the ball off himself and so it should be a corner to Reading. Those dear dead days of sportsmanship – the term 'friendly' actually meant something then!

The Women's Page was becoming more daring and cosmopolitan (with a small 'c'). They offered advice to those holidaying abroad:

> Do remember that you are, in fact, an ambassador for Britain wherever you go. . . . it is a temptation sometimes to go away in the oldest and shabbiest things, which is rather a pity. The tradition is dying hard that we are a dowdy nation, in

spite of the good work being done by our haute couture houses. . . . at least take the trouble to have your suit, dustcoat or raincoat cleaned before you visit the continent.

In these days before sunlamps were widely available, it was not considered fashionable to retain a suntan once the summer months had passed. Come September, the Women's Page offered hints on how to cover up the remains of your tan and make yourself pale and interesting for the winter. But one thing that did come back across the Channel from the foreign holidays was a taste for foreign food. The Ladies' Page made its first tentative forays into continental cuisine, with recipes for mushrooms *à la provençale* (only using half a clove of garlic) and an Italian dish described as Lasagne Casserole, in which macaroni substituted for lasagne and cottage cheese for mozzarella.

The minority Labour Government could survive no longer and a General Election was called for 25 October. The Liberals decided this time not to stand in the two Reading seats. It was the same pattern as last year. The paper painted its pen portraits of the candidates. In Mikardo's case the pen was dipped in vitriol. He was 'above all, a fighter . . . he refuses to admit defeat,

Nye Bevan speaks at the Majestic – but not everyone seems enthralled by his oratory.

Reading town centre was regularly taken over by lunacy on the day of the Rag processions in the 1950s.

even when fully justified in doing so'. His opponent, Mr H.A. Pryce, should have gone direct to 10 Downing Street, if his write-up in the paper was to be believed:

> He has the 'common touch' which makes him thoroughly at home with all classes and, a sense of justice being one of his most outstanding virtues, he detests class warfare. Sincere, steady, unemotional, Mr Pryce is no idealistic dreamer. He prefers sound planning, progress on the right lines, foresight coupled with common sense – in other words, he is typical of the modern Tory.

Heavyweight politicians were brought in to help the candidates in these two marginal seats – Harold Macmillan and Lord Hailsham spoke for the Conservatives, while Nye Bevan came to promote Labour's cause. Little notice was taken of the Labour candidate for Coventry, who turned up at Newtown School to speak for Ian Mikardo, but Richard Crossman was later to become famous as a cabinet minister and diarist.

At the election, the result nationally went to the Conservatives, but in Reading the honours were divided. Mikardo retained his seat by about a thousand votes, while Reading North went to Mr F.M. Bennett for the Conservatives, with a wafer-thin majority of just over 300. 'Half a loaf better than no bread', the *Chronicle* declared. Such was the excitement of the crowds outside the town hall that it was ten minutes before Mikardo was able to make his victory speech.

In these days before betting shops and the National Lottery, gambling was frowned upon. Fines totalling £60 were imposed upon the licencee and customers of the Red Lion in Southampton Street for the passing of betting slips. Not even charitable enterprises were exempt. An ex-policeman ran a Derby lottery at the Council's Transport Department. It raised £34, which was to be used to establish a benevolent fund for the ambulance service. However, the organiser was fined £1 and the judge ordered the proceeds to be donated to an entirely different charity.

The residents of the Field Road area of Coley were engaged in a lottery of an entirely different nature. They went to bed each night wondering if they would wake up at the bottom of a hole. Twenty years before, an entire garden shed had disappeared overnight into a hole and the situation was getting rapidly worse. Properties were having to be demolished or abandoned, and those that remained often leaned at crazy angles. In one house, the fireplace was 18 inches above the level of the adjoining floor. In another, the occupier stepped outside his back door one morning to find himself on the edge of a hole 8 feet wide and 12 feet deep. Rumours abounded of the area being honeycombed with secret Roman tunnels, but the rather more prosaic official explanation was that the houses were built on an unconsolidated rubbish tip. Needless to say, the residents approached the problem with the same calm resignation that had seen them through the war and its aftermath.

Christmas came and went, though it came rather earlier than usual when Heelas welcomed Santa, along with the Dagenham Girl Pipers and (for some unknown reason) the March Hare on 2 November. The Co-op was not far

The effects of subsidence in Field Road.

behind, with Santa's magic caterpillar ride. This provoked the Chamber of Commerce to complain about the extension of the festive season for commercial purposes. Heelas remained unabashed, reporting the best Christmas sales since before the war; Enid Blyton and the adventures of Biggles were particularly good sellers among children's books. The views of shop assistant Doreen Stone, who was roped into spending the months leading up to Christmas dressed as the March Hare, are not recorded.

THREE

1952: The King Dies

The new year brought with it an opportunity to be Miss Reading 1952. This was the first time the prewar competition had been revived. The winner would be chosen on the basis of beauty, deportment and personality by a panel including a film star, a radio presenter and a former beauty queen, at the Berkshire Press Ball in February. First, the contestants' photographs had to pass the scrutiny of a panel of local judges and there was a series of semi-finals at the local cinemas. The contest was eventually won by Anne Savage, an eighteen-year-old telephonist from Norris Road. Among her prizes were a complete new outfit, a day out meeting the stars at Pinewood Film Studios and a week's holiday at a Butlin's holiday camp. She also spent much of the summer as a minor celebrity, appearing at local events for the press photographer. It also resulted in sackfuls of fan mail, requests for pin-ups and at least two proposals of marriage.

Competitions seemed to be the flavour of the month. Later in January, the *Chronicle* launched a sewing contest for the amateur dressmaker, part of a national contest. There were six classes for different types of garment, and the winner not only received a cash prize, but also saw their creation modelled at a plush London hotel.

If sewing contests had overtones of wartime 'make do and mend', the Savings Week campaign launched in March was very like the fund-raising efforts of the war years. The theme this time was 'Lend Strength to Britain' and Reading was set the task of raising £100,000, through a whole range of organised events.

One relic of wartime that finally vanished in 1952 was the identity card. The number on it continued in use for the purpose of National Health registration, and people were advised to make a note of it before disposing of their cards, in case they subsequently had difficulty getting NHS treatment. At the same time, another relic of wartime was being revived. The Home Guard was being reformed and recruits were being sought in the Reading area. They were to be closely linked with the Territorial Army and would be given basic infantry training. However, their role was to be purely domestic – there was no danger of them being sent off to Korea, or any of the world's other trouble spots. This was just as well, given that their initial issue of equipment was limited to a tin hat and an armband. Anyone aged 18 to 65 and reasonably fit could join up.

The Vice-Chancellor of Reading University, Mr J.F. Wolfenden, officially opened the council's latest showpiece school, The Hill in Emmer Green. In his speech, he reflected upon the contrast between the facilities this school offered with those he had known as a pupil some thirty-five years earlier. This gave the editorial column another opportunity to embark on one of its favourite themes:

> Whatever its drawbacks, the Vice-Chancellor is assuredly an excellent example of a system whereby at least one of the glittering prizes was available for the talented and the industrious. Would Mr Wolfenden have us believe that his success in life was hindered by classrooms with graded floors, draughty corridors, poor ventilation and indifferent sanitation? And does he seriously contend that the more money spent on buildings the greater the profit to the state in those virtues which make for good citizenship? We have our doubts. Just as sleep heeds not a broken bed, the true content of education will never depend upon the splendour of the accommodation and the prodigality of the equipment. Ask the Scotsman!

They did not quite reach the point of saying that typhoid from the inadequate drains and pneumonia from the draughts is character-building in a pupil.

Another piece of civic spending the paper campaigned against was the proposal to build a new civic centre to the west of St Mary's Butts. This proposal had first surfaced in the council in 1946, almost thirty years before the civic centre itself was eventually to open, and the paper had condemned it then as a waste of money. More to the point, they saw it as more socialist 'big government', since it appeared to encompass plans for making Reading the seat of a new tier of regional government.

The paper favoured providing any additional space the council needed on the bombed site next to the existing town hall (that is, when they were not proposing it for a car park). Again, they brought the drains into it, citing the case a century before of the council throwing out a plan to improve the town's drainage on the grounds of cost. The same fate should befall this latest proposal, they argued. It was undoubtedly true that the council's scheme would disrupt a lot of people, requiring as it did the removal of 400 houses (only 128 of which were unfit), along with 39 industries, 97 shops, a school and 5 places of worship.

Later in the year, the first draft of the Reading Town Map – the town-planning blueprint for the Borough for the next twenty years – was published. It included the civic centre proposals and it appeared to be controversy over these that delayed the plan's submission to the Ministry. It was eventually resolved by a new proposal to replace the civic centre on a site bounded by London Road, Sidmouth Street and Eldon Road, next to Kendrick School.

The paper bade the old civic centre proposals a far from fond farewell. Among the other ideas in the plan was one for a road linking the Queens Road/London Street junction to the place (at the rear of modern-day Heelas) where Minster Street becomes Gun Street. This was seen as a way of easing traffic congestion in Broad Street, but one which could also eventually form part of an inner ring road, linking in to Castle Street, Oxford Road and Caversham Road.

Reading Football Club enjoyed one of its most successful seasons since the war, finishing up as runners-up in the Third Division (South) and scoring no fewer than 112 goals in 46 league games. They were averaging gates of over 16,000. When league leaders Plymouth came to Reading, people queued from early in the morning to get into the ground. There were over 28,000 in Elm Park when the police ordered the club to shut the turnstiles, and the queues still stretched back as far as Prospect Park. The lucky ones saw Reading win 2–0.

The star of the team, managed by former Arsenal and England player Ted Drake, was Ron Blackman. He had joined Reading as an amateur in 1946/47 and became a regular member of the first team in the middle of the 1948/49 season. In his first 133 first team appearances he scored no fewer than 101 goals for the club. He finished the 1951/52 season with a record tally of 40, including all five goals in Reading's 5–2 victory over Southend.

One of the highlights of the season was a friendly with the first division Blackpool team in which Stanley Matthews played (Blackpool won 4–2). Their manager was an ex-Reading player and the match was a testimonial for Blackman and some other first team players. Ted Drake chose the same week to announce that he was leaving to manage Chelsea. During the close season there were calls from the fans for the club to splash out anything up to £30,000 on one or two really good players. However, the only investment that the club made for the new season was in a new set of shiny 'sateen-look' shorts, which excited much ridicule in the days before sportswear had anything to do with fashion.

Football was also suffering from an outbreak of regulation. A new Entertainments Tax was expected to add something like £5,000 to Reading Football Club's bills, and could force admission charges up to the unheard-of levels of 1s 9d or even 2s! Other proposals under consideration included a ceiling of £15,000 on transfer fees for players and an increase in the maximum player's wage of £20 a week.

The king's health had been causing concern for some time and on 7 February Buckingham Palace announced that he had died. The paper carried its own editorial tribute, edged in black:

On Wednesday morning, with a suddenness that stunned the intelligence, the nation learned of the death of the King. His passing was peaceful. Unhappily, it synchronised with the absence from England of his elder daughter, the Heir to the Throne, to whom, but a few short days ago, and with a long, lingering look, he had waved farewell on her journey to distant lands as his emissary of goodwill. . . . It is a tribute to the native character of the British race that, while monarchs have fallen like autumn leaves in Europe in the last few decades, the British throne has stood like a rock; it is equally a tribute to the Royal Family that by their sterling qualities and understanding the Crown has become the symbol of an ideal democracy and a model for less discerning lands. . . . By the hand of coincidence, the new Queen has been called upon to assume the regal dignity at the same age as her illustrious predecessor, Elizabeth I, who, at Tilbury, when the great Armada was approaching the shores of England, assured her loving people that although she had but the 'body of a weak and feeble woman' she yet had the 'heart of a king'. Elizabeth II comes to her task not wholly unprepared. . . . Now she takes up the sceptre in an era with difficulties as many and problems as searching as any that faced her puissant namesake nearly four centuries ago. It is a truly heavy task and all will wish that, under divine guidance, her reign may be long and peaceful and that both she and her consort may be blessed in their endeavours.

The death of King George VI and the succession of Queen Elizabeth II is proclaimed outside the Town Hall.

The proclamation of a new queen was made outside Reading Town Hall. There were complaints that the public address system had been inaudible. A two-minute silence was ordered throughout the town and a memorial service was arranged in St Laurence's Church to coincide with the state funeral at Windsor. There were doubts for a time as to whether the University Rag Week festivities should go ahead in the midst of all this, but the mayor was mindful of their charitable function and advised that they should.

It was a mark of the high esteem in which the royal family was held at this time that even a left-wing Labour MP like Ian Mikardo should speak in Parliament in favour of the proposed Civil List for paying them salaries. Had the Bill come to Parliament fifty years ago, he said, there would have been a considerable expression of republican feeling – but not today. For once, the editorial column agreed with him: 'The Monarchy was closer to the people and stood higher in their regard, than at any time when they had been surrounded by pageantry, pomp and circumstance'.

The Women's Page unhappily chose the sombre week of the king's death to run a feature on Roger, the talking dog from Tilehurst. Roger, a regular favourite at children's parties, could drink from a baby's bottle and play football (in each case dressed in the appropriate outfit), pick out coloured blocks, perform balancing acts and say 'I want some'. (Animal lovers may be pleased to note that Roger later got his revenge for being subjected to all this, giving his owner a bite requiring four stitches during one performance.)

On a more serious note, the Women's Page celebrated Reading leading the way in the appointment of a woman to a senior position in the Trade Union movement. Reading NALGO (the local government union) had appointed the union's first female branch secretary – Mrs M.L. Gates, a clinic nurse at Grovelands School. Later in the year, the Conservatives also nominated a woman, Mrs Marjorie Hickling, to be their candidate to stand against Ian Mikardo at the next election.

The spring brought freak weather. A snowstorm in April brought traffic to a halt, wiped out the weekend sport and brought out the sledgers and skiers in force. Gale force winds blew in the window of Wellsteed's department store, hailstones the size of eggs were reported and an inch of rain caused a landslip on the railway at Winnersh, which a passenger train missed running into by just 15 yards.

Men's fashion started to feature more prominently – but in the Women's Page:

> The time is long overdue for drastic changes in male clothing. . . . there are welcome indications on all sides of a breakaway from the drabness which has chained men since the Victorian era . . . but the womanly influence can speed the process immensely. Men hate to appear conspicuous, though secretly they may yearn for wide-brimmed hats and gay fancy waistcoats, bright blue or crimson jackets or loosely flowing 'plus four' type trousers.
>
> Which brings me to a point I have often stressed. If our men are to develop their colour consciousness and dress accordingly, we shall have to be more on our toes than ever in these respects affecting ourselves – and not only while we are physically young. Far too many British women let themselves go when they pass the thirty mark, when in point of fact, with proper care, they may pass to a charm which the younger and less experienced must envy. It is all a question of foundation – corsetry by experts.

The fears of the Women's Page seem unfounded to us today. Dressed as they describe, their menfolk are more likely to be invited to join a circus than run off with another woman. In another edition, this new liberalism in men's fashion manifested itself in the horrifying form of the Television Jacket:

> Made in fine barathea, its long curved revers and three-quarter cuffs are silk faced and there is a single button-link fastening. This leisure garment sells at about ten guineas and the best of the various colours is a rich maroon. The jacket's elegant, easy lines make it perfect for slipping on for an evening at home.

Did people really dress up like Noel Coward for an evening in front of the box? On a rather more utilitarian note:

> A new article of menswear which will find favour with wives is a plastic collar, wiped clean with a damp cloth twice a week. It is comfortable to wear and cuts household laundry bills. The collar will last for about two months and is then thrown away.

The town's traffic problems continued to exercise many minds. The mayor, speaking at a road safety committee, thought that one-way traffic should be tried on some of the town's streets. He also wanted to see special lay-bys provided for buses, to prevent them queueing in the middle of the road to pick up passengers and holding up traffic. One member of the committee came up with the idea of putting bumps in the road to slow down traffic at danger spots, but the idea was dismissed as impracticable.

The town's Chief Constable, Mr J. Lawrence, was more concerned with the safety of individual vehicles and their drivers. He put forward some radical ideas in his annual report:

> A motor vehicle is a lethal weapon, yet the majority of drivers today have had only a slipshod and haphazard course of initial driving instruction, and I do feel that consideration of introducing legislation governing driving tuition, examination and subsequent re-examination is long overdue. Such legislation might be coupled with regulations to authorise the periodic inspection and certification of roadworthiness of vehicles for, in these days of short supply in the new car market, old cars are being retained when their performance has reached a dangerously low level of efficiency.

A Government White Paper caused the paper to look back fondly to an old solution to Reading's transport problems:

> Last year, according to the Government's recent White Paper on transport policy, 12 million tons of cargo were carried on the canals, a tithe of what would be possible if all the waterways were working to capacity. For the bulk carriage of such commodities as coal, grain and oil, the canals are still the cheapest. . . . Just over a century ago, the value to Reading of the Kennet and Avon Canal could be measured by the fact that 20,000 sacks of flour were sent to London each year, and in 1835 it was estimated that, of the annual import and export trade of Reading, 50,000 tons were waterborne and 100 tons went by road. . . . it was just when the canals were at the peak of their usefulness that the railway came. How often now does one see a laden barge passing under High Bridge? And how long is it since one reached Bristol?

The prospects of any serious canal traffic along the Kennet & Avon were remote indeed. The Docklands and Inland Waterways Executive announced that they were going to do some essential repairs along the Reading/Newbury stretch. Their survey had identified such problems as collapsed weirs and lock gates that had been seized shut for years. Also in 1952, plans to create riverside walkways along 136 miles of the River Thames were rejected on grounds of cost. It was said that such a path would cost at least £60,000 a year to maintain.

The new council houses on the Bath Road estate started to become available. The first one, on Silchester Road, went to a couple who, with their two children, had spent ten years of their married life in rented rooms. At the Ideal Homes Exhibition in London, the People's Houses were displayed. Designed by the Government to be cheap, quick and easy to build, they featured such amenities

Many thought the Kennet & Avon Canal's future lay with commercial traffic, but this salt barge was a comparative rarity.

Leisure boating was to provide the real future for the Kennet & Avon Canal.

as built-in cupboards and cookers. Also much vaunted at the exhibition was the use of fitted carpets and full-length mirrors to create the illusion of space. Possibly the most unusual gadget on display there was one that attached to your vacuum cleaner and for £4 13s 6d would convert your sink into a washing machine and dishwasher (one assumes not at the same time).

The Women's Page ran a feature on how to furnish a three-bedroom flat for £190, which contained a couple of interesting assumptions for the modern reader: 'Kitchen equipment is not included in the budget since most flat dwellers share a kitchen and a few essentials such as a table lamp or an electric fire are assumed as wedding presents.'

For those living at the bottom of the housing market, conditions could be positively dangerous. No. 57 Weldale Street was a shop with a lodging house above. One night, one of the lodgers awoke to find the building ablaze. He was able to escape, using a rope of knotted sheets, and raised the alarm. When the fire brigade got there, they found other residents hanging out of the first floor windows and four men unconscious in the upper rooms. They got all four out but only two survived. The fire was blamed on a cigarette end falling down into a chair.

One group which could look forward to improved housing in 1952 were those moving into the new council children's home, at Monksbarn in Cressingham Road. The council had bought the ten-bedroom house with 11 acres, and the cost of keeping a child there was estimated at £6 5s 9d per week. Mr J.L. West, the Chairman of the Children's Committee, was afraid that its comparative luxury might give the children false ideas.

The criminal classes could still be relied upon to give splendid displays of incompetence. One man who broke into the Arborfield British Legion left behind two shirt buttons and a piece of paper bearing his name and address. He was arrested before he could get home and change his shirt and got two years for the theft of drinks and cigarettes. In another case, the police raided the house of a man suspected of breaking into a grocer's shop. They found his wife in bed, but noticed that her pillow was very hard and lumpy. It was found to have chocolate biscuits sewn into it!

The police had a new weapon in their fight against crime (though, with criminals like those above, they hardly needed it). Wireless communication was being installed between their headquarters and their patrol cars. Initially, six of Reading's police cars were to be equipped in this way. Linked to the use of the 999 emergency number, it could ensure a rapid response to serious problems. But the public had still not quite got the hang of the purpose of the 999 number. It was regularly used to report the finding of stray dogs and one woman used it to report seeing a squirrel on her clothes-line post!

The government announced in Parliament that the BBC's monopoly of television broadcasting was to end, leading the paper to speculate about its consequences:

> The question of the competitive element in what has hitherto been a strict monopoly naturally aroused a minor conflict of opinion, for many, apart from their political views, fear a lowering of the quality of television programmes and the introduction of the farrago of blatant advertising which is loosed over the air on the American network, despite the assurance of the Home Secretary that their fears are groundless. 'We have our typical ways of resolving problems of taste, just like any other problems. We are a much more mature and sophisticated people.'

A sample of the bizarre entertainment on offer at the Palace – the phrase 'politically correct' had yet to be coined.

A favourite Christmas present for 1950s children.

In the course of his brief for the opposition Mr Morrison mentioned the case of an engine driver who resigned his seat on the Town Council because of the home lure of the television. Here is posed a question far more important than the issues discussed in the House. The day is obviously not far distant when it will no longer be necessary to venture forth on a cold winter's night to hear the impassioned oratory of eminent political folk – they will obligingly come into the snug, warm sitting room and say their piece with the traditional appeal and gesture. The effect, also of the growing competition of television in other fields cannot be underrated.

Commercial television had no need of licence fees, but a new technological breakthrough was being used against the estimated 200,000 households nationwide suspected of viewing without a licence. Demonstrations of television detector vans were held locally, warning people of the hefty £100 fine and confiscation of the set for licence evasion. One of the trial's more interesting findings – possibly highlighting the status attached to owning a television in those days – was that a significant number of people had had an aerial put on their houses without actually buying a set!

In the live theatre, one of the year's finest examples of 'the show must go on' spirit came from Miss Betty Allen, better known to her devotees as 'Roxana', the snake dancer. While waiting to go on at the Palace Theatre, her 10-foot python sank its fangs into her and tried to crush her. She was rescued by two assistants, who wrestled the beast from her and got it back into its cage. After a visit to hospital to have the wound dressed, she returned to the Palace with a bandaged arm and performed her act, collapsing as the curtain went down. The condition of the snake was not reported.

As if this were not excitement enough for one year, 1952 also featured Herring Week. Highlights of this included window displays by fishmongers and a Kipper Breakfast at the George Hotel, at which celebrities including the mayor and Ian Mikardo lavished praise upon this noble denizen of the deep. The purpose of it all was to get everyone to eat more herrings. It was calculated that every man, woman and child needed to eat three more herrings a week to ease the recession in the fishing industry.

So ended 1952. And as Miss Reading 1952 answered the last of her fan mail, the search began for Miss Reading 1953.

FOUR

1953: Coronation

The new year came in relatively quietly in Reading. Local licensing rules closed Reading's pubs at 11.00 p.m., so many of the most serious revellers decanted to hostelries outside the Borough, which were allowed to stay open to see in the new year. Others saved their energies for the new year's sales, where a buying spree was reported. Among the bargains to catch the editorial eye were beaver lamb fur coats for 12 guineas and three piece suites from £39 10s. Redina, whose byline appeared on the Women's Page, offered her readers a series of new year's resolutions. They included the following gems:

Laugh at your friends' jokes, even if you've heard them before;
Keep the day for your children, the evening for your husband;
Don't bore your husband with a recital of the day's trivialities – be ready to listen to him instead;
Keep one night for yourself – your hair, your beauty, your hands, your wardrobe. The family can have the rest of the week;
Don't be witty at someone else's expense; and
Wipe the kitchen shelves once a week.

In another memorable feature, Redina devoted virtually the entire column to a detailed explanation of how to do the weekly clothes wash, for the benefit of the newlywed wife. And a prewar favourite began to make a comeback on the dining table:

And so the white loaf is coming back. It will gladden the heart of those who remember it in the dim and distant days before the war and if it costs a little more, it will be gladly paid.

The town's plans to celebrate the coronation began to emerge early in the year. Unlike their efforts for the Festival of Britain, the council threw itself into this event with enthusiasm. A budget of £9,000 was set aside for it and the inevitable committee formed. Every primary schoolchild was to receive a commemorative teaspoon, and a Queen Elizabeth II Coronation Prize Fund was to be endowed for secondary school children. One of the town's foster homes was to be given a television set to enable them to watch the coronation. Public buildings were to

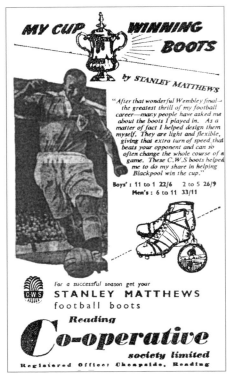

An early example of a sporting personality being used in merchandising.

Every advertiser tried to cash in on the coronation.

be decorated and the Forbury Gardens floodlit. Fairy lights were being hung in the Forbury Gardens, Christchurch playing fields, Thameside Promenade and Caversham Court. There were to be band concerts, a procession and fireworks, and the Rotary Club was installing televisions in the town hall to enable elderly people to watch the event.

But, before the coronation, the town experienced a no less joyful, but rather less dignified, celebration. Previous University Rag Days had seen some tension between town and gown, with allegations of vandalism flying about. But this year's event was reckoned to be one of the biggest and best ever. During the day, the parade through the town centre brought traffic to a standstill. A mock police patrol car, conducting a comic 'chase' of some criminals, nearly caused an accident when a smoke canister hanging underneath it fell off and rolled under a nearby parked car. This filled Broad Street with choking fumes and threatened to set the car alight, until a policeman retrieved it. The other floats displayed the good taste for which student rags are renowned, with a torture chamber and the time-honoured blood transfusion among the tableaux. The whole town centre was given over to temporary insanity, as people played marbles with glass eyes among the traffic, anglers fished down drains, bacon frying took place on traffic islands and a spoof medicine man sold patent remedies in Market Place. Reading residents shared the pavements with a twenty-legged dragon, a chain gang, Ku Klux Klansmen with a bomb and a slave girl auction where the prices started at 2s. The evening was given over to a torchlight procession to Hills Meadow, where an estimated 12,000 people assembled for an evening of mediaeval fun, with roast venison on a spit, jousting, single combat, archery and morris dancing.

Not all the members of the student body were in favour of this foolishness. The newspaper received the following message, complete with capital letters and inverted commas:

> NOT ALL Reading students approved of the scandalous and immodest behaviour of particular individuals in regard to the recent 'rag'. 'Rags' are ALLEGED to be for charitable purposes; the veil of 'charity' can indeed fairly be used to cover activities of a GROTESQUE nature, but NOT to cover indecency.

Evil influences of another kind caused a great deal of interest locally. The BBC broadcast a radio programme from the South Reading Community Centre, in which the audience and a panel of experts discussed the baleful influence of comics – especially American-type comics – upon young people. The panel included the publishers of such works as the *Roy Rogers Comic*, *Hopalong Cassidy* and *Six Gun Heroes*, as well as an authoress not widely known for her portrayals of violence and depravity – Enid Blyton. Some of the people best placed to comment were excluded – there was a ban on children under fourteen attending.

Enid Blyton was especially opposed to the science fiction comics showing monsters: 'These are pictures drawn by men who must have depraved minds. I never put anything frightening in my books, for if I did I would get thousands of letters from parents.' The paper supported her stand:

> There is a growing feeling that the increase in juvenile crime is, at least in part, attributed to the lurid presentation of what are termed 'the comics'; that the derring-do conveyed by this means to the child's mind is vastly different from that of 'Treasure Island' and 'Westward Ho!' or even Sexton Blake or even the thrilling Marvels that may have been nostalgically remembered by some of the male audience of riper years on the occasion of the broadcast.
>
> There seems to be a consensus of opinion – apart from the views of the zealous devotees of an enlarged freedom for the young – that the new form of picturisation is coming to the youthful mind in an extravagant and dangerous form, promoting unhealthy cravings which lie deep in the mind and have not been wholly exorcised by the thin veneer of a civilisation only a few thousand years old. . . .
>
> [T]wo great world conflicts have unleashed a strange unrest which is permeating every phase of the social order. Its manifestations are apparent in art and music and more dangerous channels. It would be a natural disaster if these disordered imaginings were to be nourished at a tender age with the connivance of commerce and the approval of the parents.

And I always thought Hopalong Cassidy was one of the good guys. Fears of corruption and depravity appeared to be endemic in the Reading of 1953. In the same month, the Reading and District Baptist Council called for the banning of the film *One Summer of Happiness*, which contained a nude bathing scene. One of the councillors, a Mr F.W. Button, stood out against the general outrage, warning that they should not judge the film unseen:

> The Council should not do this without a first-hand knowledge of the film. . . .
> a member of the Council should be asked to see the film in London and let the
> Council have his views.

However, the Revd Mr Webb decided to spare Mr Button, or anyone else, from this distasteful duty, by seeking the views of the Public Morality Council in London. It was agreed that, if they disapproved, the Baptist Council would lobby the Watch Committee for the film to be banned in Reading.

But, if anything needed to be banned, it was some of the lurid colour schemes emerging from the Ideal Homes Exhibition. It was reported that the most popular furnishing colour there was lime green, especially when matched with strong tones such as royal blue, cherry, yellow and burgundy. In an inspired combination of health and beauty, they also recommended pinboards, in these colours and made out of asbestos, for the children's bedrooms.

As if in punishment for all this wickedness, Reading was subjected to a 'bombing raid' in which some 500 tons of bombs (more than destroyed Coventry during the war) fell on an area of the town centred around the railway station. Fortunately, this all took place in the fertile minds of the civil defence planners. The emergency services were given the details of the bombing patterns and assumptions about damage and casualties, and were called upon to plan their response.

One place where the police were required to act for real was a scene of triumph, rather than disaster. 'Syncopating Sandy', the mystery man from Bolton, chose Palmer Hall in West Street as the venue for his attempt on the non-stop piano-playing record of 130 hours (then held by a German, as the paper pointedly mentioned). As he neared the conclusion of his successful bid, sustained by gallons of tea and 200 cigarettes, the crowds flocking to see him grew so dense that police reinforcements had to be brought in to control them. Afterwards, he still had enough energy to sign autographs before departing for an engagement in America.

Council house building hit new heights. Nearly two new council homes were being completed each day – 660 in the year. Cllr Hammond said that the Conservative party was carrying out its pledges. They had freed the private housebuilder from regulation and brought in a scheme for council tenants to buy houses on easy terms. This scheme was later reported to be a failure, with only thirty-five properties being bought in Reading in the first year. The house building programme itself was not without its difficulties. The new Southcote estate suffered from an epidemic of vandalism. Houses awaiting letting had their rooms flooded, fires started in the rooms and their windows smashed. No doubt the local youth had been reading too many comics.

One family became the occupiers of two council houses. Mr and Mrs Downs had been living in a three-bedroom terraced house with no electricity, no bath and only one toilet, along with their twelve children aged between two and twenty-one. They had been on the council house waiting list for seven years, with their seven daughters sleeping in three double beds in one bedroom, four boys in another and the couple themselves and their youngest child in a third. They were given two adjoining council houses, knocked together, prompting the paper to ask if this was Reading's biggest family.

It was not. The Robbins family of Brigham Road had seventeen children in their four-bedroom house, and had not even made it to the top of the waiting list. Their £4 a week family allowance helped to pay for the 65 pints of milk and 25s worth of bread they consumed every week.

Equally productive in his own way was a father of nine children from Foxhays Road, described as a 41-year-old traveller. His procreative activities had to be confined to the weekends, since he travelled during the week to another 'wife', who also had a child by him. He left her on Fridays, on the pretext of visiting his sick father, but eventually appeared before the courts on a charge of bigamy.

As the coronation approached, the paper was filled with pages about the royal family and the preparations, both in Reading and in London. A competition was launched to find Reading's best decorated streets and people went to extraordinary lengths to outdo each other. One woman – a Mrs Jones of Filey Road – constructed a balcony, complete with cutouts of the royal family, on the front of her house. In the winning street, Amity Road, the residents clubbed together to raise over £100 towards the cost of the decorations and, even where

Amity Road won the coronation street decorations prize.

less money was available, ingenuity and hard work produced some striking results.

Public buildings throughout the town centre were decorated – the town hall was decked out with a picture of the queen and flags of all nations, and Heelas wore a huge crown. But the most striking feature of the coronation was the evidence that the television age had truly arrived:

> In Reading, the 'writing on the wall' was unmistakable; television has practically killed public celebrations on a general scale. Organisers must in future make their arrangements in complete deference to the lure of the magic window which opens up such amazing possibilities.

The Borough Council's ambitious programme of local events attracted only a meagre response from the public. This may have had something to do with the bad weather on the day but, by contrast, the town hall was packed with far more than the thousand pensioners who had been invited. There, giant television screens had been erected for them to watch the events in London. Many of them were seeing television for the first time.

The procession through the town centre was one event which attracted a reasonable crowd. Among the floats which, according to the paper 'attracted gasps of admiration and applause' from the crowd, was the *Chronicle*'s own Tableau of Beauty. This featured not only Miss Reading 1953 and her runner-up, but also the former Miss Reading 1952, who was no longer Miss Savage but Mrs Johansen. The coronation swimming contest at Thamesside

Newtown crowns its own Coronation Queen.

The town hall, floodlit for the coronation.

Ukraine temporarily joins the Commonwealth, as Reading people from all nations celebrate the coronation.

Promenade took place despite the weather, though some events had to be cancelled owing to a lack of women swimmers. At various high points around the borough, troops of damp boy scouts attempted to light their links in a chain of commemorative bonfires. And, by night, four hundred people at the Olympia ballroom danced at the Coronation Ball to the music of Don Turk and his band.

Reading Council also celebrated the 700th anniversary of the granting of their first royal charter, by Henry III in 1253 (although someone had subsequently mislaid it). They applied to the College of Heralds for additions to their coat of arms and held an exhibition of their surviving sixteen charters in the town hall. For any heraldry enthusiasts reading this, the additions to the crest consisted of two rams argent as supporters, a crest in the form of a bishop's mitre and the motto 'A deo et regina'.

Two extremes of motoring achievement were celebrated by the paper in the same week in June. A Wokingham man, Duncan Hamilton, was one of the drivers of the winning Jaguar XK120 at the Le Mans 24 hour sports car race. They covered 2,440 miles in the course of the 24 hours, the first team ever to average over 100mph for the entire race. Hamilton, an ex-Fleet Air Arm pilot and successful businessman, was off the following weekend to enter his own Jaguar in the Portugese Grand Prix (these being the days when the gentleman amateur did not have to contend with the might of the sponsored teams).

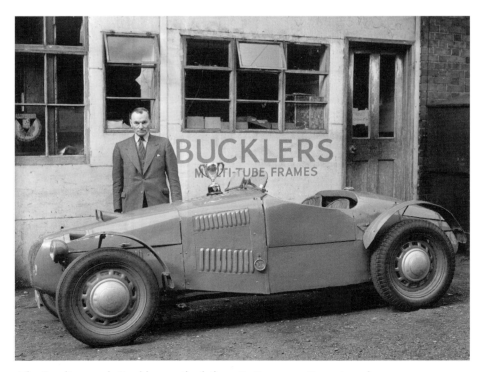

The Reading-made Buckler car, fresh from its Economy Run triumph.

Hillman stretch their cars – and the credulity of their readers. But Reliant had no need of artistic licence to improve their sleek outlines.

A Reading-built car – the Buckler, built by Derek Buckler of Woodcote Road – achieved the other triumph, covering a 600-mile course at a more stately 30 mph. His home-made car used an engine from a clapped-out Ford van, but he still averaged 91 mpg in the National Road Fuel Economy Contest.

The Motor Show prompted great interest locally, as new cars became more readily available. A total of thirty-one British makes were on display – with lost names such as Allard, Alvis, Armstrong Siddeley, Frazer Nash, Jowett and Lanchester among them. The surprise of the show was the new Ford Popular, the cheapest postwar car at £275 (plus £115 14s 2d purchase tax). Despite its low price, this was no austerity model, the paper assured us. The 1,172cc engine produced no less than 30bhp and its long list of standard features (not optional extras, you will note) included bumpers, hub caps, a spare wheel and a real boot you could open from the outside.

The drawings of their cars used by many manufacturers in their advertisements would not have stood the scrutiny of a modern Advertising Standards Authority. The dumpiest of small saloons was elongated and streamlined to an almost unrecognisable degree, while anything approaching an average family saloon was made to look more like a top of the market American import.

The *Chronicle* wanted to know what the Reading public thought of the prospect of 'sponsored television' (as they then called the forthcoming commercial channel). Opinions were widely divided. Some doubted the value of television of any description. As one woman put it:

I can't get on with anything. My husband and the children sit on the floor and won't move, there has to be strict silence, friends and neighbours are always coming in to share the set and they occupy every chair. I wish television had never been invented.

A larger group were willing to give it a trial. One interviewee said his family had now got over the novelty of television – they had become discriminating: 'If we do not want to look in at any particular feature, we turn to sound radio. It is common sense to have both where possible.'

Possibly the most Luddite view came from a cinema manager, who held that the place for television was in cinemas and public halls, not in the home. In fact, the long decline of the cinema had begun, despite their best efforts to win back the crowds with novelties such as 3D films like *The House of Wax* with Vincent Price. Among the other stars on the screen that year were Joan Collins (not a child star, even in those days) and, playing a red-necked shoot-'em-down US marshal in *Law and Order*, someone called Ronald Reagan. (Whatever became of him?)

Another woman prospective parliamentary candidate was chosen, this time by Labour for Reading North. Mrs Pat Llewelyn-Davies was a graduate of Girton College, Cambridge, and had been a former candidate against Enoch Powell in Wolverhampton, but the paper none the less insisted on describing her as 'a vivacious 38, brown of hair and eyes, slimly petite'. Why were we denied such essential details about Ian Mikardo?

At Elm Park, it was rumoured that the club might get floodlights. This led to fears that they might be tempted to play too many games and overtax the stamina of their players. There were also questions about whether the investment would be worthwhile, since the football authorities did not allow League matches to be played under lights.

Bulls department store in Broad Street closed, with a party for four hundred present and former staff. The building was sold and the business taken over by Heelas, which had recently become part of the John Lewis Partnership.

The Schools Medical Officer reported that many Berkshire school buildings were unsanitary. Berkshire had the lowest spending on school buildings of any local authority in the country. A creative solution to the problem was proposed – don't send the children to school! Pupils aged over thirteen were allowed to take up to ten half-days off, to help with potato picking in the light of labour shortages on the farms. In Reading itself, the rate of housing growth was outstripping the capacity of the schools. There were now 16,603 pupils but only 16,181 school places. Most schools were overcrowded, some to a serious degree. One, serving a new housing estate, had 1,000 pupils crammed into the space designed for 600. Church halls and other accommodation were pressed into service to meet the shortfall and new schools – including a new secondary school on Cockney Hill – were being planned or built.

As if local housing shortages were not enough, plans were announced to relocate 5,000 'overspill' Londoners onto Reading's borders, in the Wokingham area. The paper became very exercised about this, and the planners got it in the neck again:

Overcrowding became a serious problem in Reading schools. This was Battle School in 1954.

If London wants more room for her population, why can she not build upwards? As the poet Cowper said: 'God made the country and man made the town'. There should be as little disturbance as possible in this arrangement. A feeling is growing that some of the planning zealots should be given a long holiday without pay. . . .

The proclivity of the planners to cry doom is instanced in another field. Eager statisticians have foretold that, in fifty years or less – it is the almost indecent haste of the planners that is so aggravating – the larger part of the population of the world will die of hunger. The lugubrious tabulators of woe never seem to realise that nature has its ways of adjustment which are very real, even if they appear haphazard.

Housing land was in short supply within the borough, and a proposal was made to develop large areas of Coley Park for housing, assuming it could be prised out of government ownership. The 'lugubrious tabulators of woe' were predicting that Reading would itself have an overspill population of some 9,200 by 1971.

The year would not be complete without a controversy involving Ian Mikardo, so in December he got himself censured by the Labour Party National Executive for a *Tribune* article criticising the position of the TUC on the British Guiana question. (Few can now remember what the question was, let alone what the correct answer should have been.)

Meanwhile, Father Christmas was up to his old trick of arriving early – and he was getting worse than ever! Scarcely had the last summer holidaymakers got home and unpacked when – on 31 October – Santa arrived at Reading. His

Home movies in the days before camcorders.

first manifestation was at Heelas, where he occupied a Toytown complete with pets' corner, the man in the moon and a rocket which despatched toys into outer space for some unspecified reason.

Another Father Christmas appeared shortly afterwards at Reading station. There, he boarded his giant sleigh drawn by reindeer and, accompanied by the Ercol Band, the old woman in the shoe (with all her children) and 'a tableau of the east', made his noisy way to McIlroy's toy grotto, to be greeted by the mayor. In the event, the sleigh proved to be superfluous; the Christmas was one of the mildest on record and people were able to go out without their overcoats on Christmas Day.

FIVE

1954: Teddy Boys and Tragedy

For two Polish émigrés living just outside Reading, the year began with an affectionate hug at a new year's party. But the affection was gone when, three months later, the one took the other to court. He was suing for £84 loss of earnings, following seven weeks off work with broken ribs.

Rockets to the moon may have been a feature of Heelas' toy department in the Christmas of 1953, but the real thing was a distant prospect, according to one expert in January 1954:

> Man-carrying rockets to the moon are unlikely before the turn of the century, said Dr L.R. Shepherd, Vice-President of the British Interplanetary Association, lecturing on interplanetary flight to a packed audience at Reading Town Hall on Monday.
>
> But Dr Shepherd, who is also an atomic energy research scientist at Harwell and Vice-President of the International Astronautical Federation, forecast that, within this century, rockets carrying scientific instruments would be bringing back valuable information about space and pictures of the planets taken without the blanket of the earth's atmosphere.

According to Dr Shepherd, the problems of getting a rocket to the moon could only be overcome by building a rocket capable of a speed of 50,000mph, which was not possible with known forms of propulsion. As with many problems in those days, he thought that nuclear power might hold the solution. Among his other predictions, he envisaged the creation of orbiting permanent space stations. In the event, progress was far more rapid than he had expected. Within three years of this talk, Russia had launched its first Sputnik and the space age had begun.

Two appeals were launched at the start of 1954. One was to raise £1,500 to repair the spire of St Giles' Church, which had become dangerous. The other sought to establish 'junk playgrounds' in some of the most densely built-up areas of the town. These were pockets of land, equipped with such play equipment as concrete pipes and old steamrollers, presumably for those children who could not find a real building site to risk their lives on.

Reading FC Supporters' Club had been defunct since 1948, when an argument between the club and its supporters had led to its recognition being withdrawn. Early in 1954, moves were made to revive it, and to release the assets of over £1,000 which the supporters' club had possessed when it expired. One of the highlights of the club's year was a visit by First Division (for younger readers, substitute Premier League) club Newcastle United. The club, featuring five internationals including Jackie Milburn, came to Elm Park for a testimonial for two of Reading's long-standing players, George Marks and Bill Livingstone.

Car parking on match days had already become a nightmare for people living around Elm Park. Residents of Parkside Road lobbied for Prospect Park to be used as a car park to relieve pressure on the streets near to the ground but the council was not keen on the idea.

There were ructions within the club when they sold two of their star players, Ron Blackman (to Nottingham Forest) and Stan Wicks (to Chelsea). It later emerged at the AGM that the club had had to sell players to meet debts of £29,000. They said they were being crippled by the Entertainments Tax and needed average home gates of 16,000 just to stay in the black. (They were getting fewer than 12,000 for part of the year.) They were, however, able to buy former Scottish international Bobby Campbell, also from Chelsea (managed by former Reading boss Ted Drake) and their new floodlights (better than Arsenal's, claimed some people) got their trial run in October, with a friendly against Racing Club de Paris.

The Olympia ballroom banned the practice of jiving at its Saturday night dances. This may have had something to do with the arrival of one of the first youth cults in Reading. The term 'teddy boys', by which they became better known, took a while to appear in the local paper.

'BORDERING ON RIOT' – POLICE INSPECTOR
YOUTHS IN SATURDAY NIGHT FRACAS
For some time, youths dressed in what is known as the Edwardian style have been making nuisances of themselves, particularly after dances in the town. On Saturday night, the traffic was stopped and the convenience of the public completely ignored, it being the most serious of this type of incident which has taken place in Reading for a long time. . . .

An attempt was made to overturn a police van, whilst there was damage to police clothing and their method of fighting was not such as would appeal to the average Englishman.

Some sixty youths, dressed in the Edwardian style, took part in the affray, which completely blocked the Caversham Road for a time one Saturday night. Four of them, aged between seventeen and twenty-one, appeared before the courts, receiving fines and in one case a prison sentence of six months.

For those of better character, the *Berkshire Chronicle* was giving away free money. Strangely enough, they were finding precious few takers. William Laud was the only Reading-born man ever to rise to the position of Archbishop of

Canterbury. He had been a close confidant of King Charles I (for which he was eventually executed) but had retained an active interest in his home town, setting up a charity – Archbishop Laud's gift to the Reading Corporation. This paid marriage portions of up to £50 to 'young women of good character' who were planning to wed. The lack of applicants was probably less to do with the shortage of women of good character in Reading, and more to do with the fact that they had to be in domestic service. These were a dying breed by the 1950s, and the charity had to broaden its scope to include those working in nursing or caring for parents.

Fire broke out in the Dellwood Nursery Home in April 1954. Fifteen infants, some as young as one day old, were in their cots in the main ward. The nursing staff, and Sister Freda Holland in particular, made heroic efforts to rescue their tiny charges. She suffered severe burns in the process, but as a result of her courage only one of the babies died immediately from burns. Tragically, however, smoke had entered the lungs of the others and, in the days that followed, the death toll from breathing problems rose steadily to thirteen. The two survivors were described as having no more than 'a sporting chance'.

The funeral for the victims of the Dellwood fire.

More than 300 people attended the funeral of eleven of the victims the following week. All the fathers were there, but only two of the mothers were in a fit state to attend. As the tiny coffins were lowered into the grave, one of the grief-stricken fathers collapsed and had to be helped away from the graveside.

A few weeks later, the paper was able to publish happier pictures of the survivors, nursed back to health. Sister Holland subsequently received the George Medal, and she and her colleague Sister Margaret Thomas both got awards from the Carnegie Hero Fund Trust. A complaint was made to the Press Council about the extent to which Sister Holland was being harassed by the media. The *Berkshire Chronicle* was quick to publish a disclaimer, saying that it was not them.

There was almost another tragedy in July:

TRAGEDY AVERTED BY OAK TREES
PILOTLESS JET FIGHTER CRASHES ON NURSERY
MISSES NEARBY HOUSES BY A MATTER OF YARDS
A clump of massive oak trees, bordering the Burghfield Road, undoubtedly prevented loss of life and considerable damage to houses on Sunday morning when a jet fighter, from which the pilot had baled out, crashed into some glasshouses at the Cooperative Wholesale Society's Kennet Valley Nurseries. Had the plane not struck the trees, which diverted its flight, it would most certainly have crashed on a row of small houses in front of the nurseries, where workers in the greenhouses live. The trees, with their tops now lopped, stand as a gaunt reminder of the tragedy averted.

The jet fighter – a Vampire – was on a training flight from Pembrey in Wales, and the pilot had parachuted just outside Guildford. He landed safely just outside the city.

When the aircraft landed at the nursery it exploded, wrecking some sixteen to twenty greenhouses. Wreckage was scattered over a large area. The force of the explosion blew huge lumps of coal from the side of the nursery into an adjoining field, yet strangely enough only a very small number of panes of glass . . . were broken. . . .

Not only was the crash felt many miles away, but a woman at Sulhampstead Abbots – some nine miles distant – saw from her bedroom window what she described as 'a ball of fire suddenly dip and crash'.

Eye-witnesses just yards away from the scene described seeing the plane strike the trees and plunge from the sky in a deafening explosion.

An equally unmanned locomotive made a getaway from the station in Reading and got as far as Crowthorne before it slowed enough on an incline for a driver to jump on board and bring it to a halt. Among the other transport stories of the year, calls for a helicopter pad in Reading were renewed – there were fears among some councillors that Reading was being left behind in what was seen as the coming form of transport. The deputy mayor suggested that the best site for it was in Woodley (outside the borough). The Chamber of Commerce went one better, and called for a combined rail, bus and helicopter interchange right in the heart of the town centre. Perhaps most difficult to believe, the Corporation bus company was running 'tours of the town' bus excursions for the second year. In 1953 they had found no fewer than 7,000 takers for these trips to see the wonders of Reading.

But nothing is impossible, given faith, and one man who had it in abundance was Charles William Potter. He was the Secretary of the Reading Communist Party, until he discovered God at a Billy Graham rally in London. He must have surprised many who, seeing him arrive with his regular soap box in Market Place, found him dispensing the gospel according to Jesus, rather than that of Karl Marx.

Reading's University Orchestra celebrated its golden jubilee under the distinguished baton of Sir Adrian Boult. He had actually appeared as a singer with the orchestra early in his career, and had frequently conducted them since. They too had enjoyed a distinguished history, and had been conducted for a time by Gustav Holst. Their tradition of performing works by students of the University had included one by Edmund Rubbra, who went on from Reading to study with Holst and Vaughan Williams and became a leading British composer of his day.

The question occupying some people's minds was 'what is a sausage?' Frosts the butchers of Union Street were prosecuted for selling pork chipolatas with a meat content of only 43 per cent. It was claimed by the plaintiffs that, although no formal rules existed, the convention was that the meat content should be around 65 per cent. They also said that they were not bringing the prosecution with a view to exacting a heavy penalty from the defendant – they were more interested in getting a ruling on the matter from the court for future reference. The magistrates pleased nobody, by fining Frosts £20 plus £6 13s costs, but declining to set down a ruling as to what the minimum meat content should be.

Council tenants could look forward to frying their sausages by electricity. It was decided to install it in all prewar council houses, at a cost of £53,800. The tenants would pay for the work over a fifteen-year period, by means of an extra shilling a week on their rents.

However, this also opened up the possibility of them watching commercial television, with all its attendant dangers. The Revd H.G. Owen, speaking to the Reading Temperance Society, warned that this could be one of the greatest menaces to the cause of total abstinence. He saw the evil hand of the brewing industry behind the drive for commercial television, since it would enable them to run seductive advertisements along the lines of 'beer is best', subverting the minds of Britain's youth with their siren song.

Other advertisements promised an end to 'those dreary years of making do'. Life was worth living again, as Stork margarine became available once more with the end of rationing. Meat also came off ration, but Reading saw none of the panic-buying that affected London. The only difference was that

new BLACKCURRANT SPANGLES!

SPANGLES

Here's the rich flavour of garden-ripe blackcurrants—packed for you in the handy Spangles way.
Look for the new, easy-to-undo wrappings, too!

Life's always sweeter with Spangles   3ᵈ a packet

All Fruit Flavour Spangles contain natural fruit extracts and other fine flavours.

prices went up slightly, so that New Zealand lamb cost 3s to 3s 6d a pound and rump steak 4s 6d to 5s 6d.

There was more celebration, as Heelas marked its centenary with displays of goods of yesteryear and products from around the world. They had come a long way from the small draper's shop founded in Minster Street in 1854 by Daniel Heelas. They were also involved in a debate about the dress code for their staff. Should all heads of department be required to dress in black jacket and pinstripe trousers, or could some of the more junior staff be allowed to wear conventional lounge suits (made of a material approved by the managing directors, naturally)? In the event that this confused the customers, it was suggested that the staff could wear an identifying badge.

The *Daily Express* sponsored a debate on 'You and your Wages' in Reading town hall, led by a panel of local MPs and businessmen. In the course of it, the question of a recent trade pact with Japan came up – should we be encouraging them to sell more goods to us? Mr F.M. Bennett (Reading's other MP – the uncontroversial one) supported the pact, explaining that last year, the Japanese bought £240 millions worth of goods from us, while we bought only £120 millions from them. Trade had to be two-way and an imbalance could not go on for too long. Unless the Japs (as he called them) could buy with what they made in their trading, we would lose our markets. As we later saw, there was no danger of the Japanese going broke.

International trade may be good business, but the members of Bradfield Rural District Council were beginning to have doubts that atomic war was good business, as least as far as they were concerned. Questions began to be asked about the possible health hazards posed to the local population by the Atomic Weapons Establishment at Aldermaston. A bland letter from the Ministry of Housing was read out at a council meeting, referring to the statutory duty on the establishment not to discharge dangerous radiation (as if they were going to do it on purpose). The most disturbing part of it, however, was a reference to proposals to let them make limited discharges of atomic waste into the atmosphere, subject to certain safeguards.

The Civil Defence exercise 'Operation Lowland' looked at how Reading would cope on the fringes of a nuclear holocaust. Teams of rescuers were despatched into the town to help members of the Casualties Union, dressed up as victims of an atomic bomb. No compromise was made in achieving realism. There were victims trapped under beams and others buried under piles of rubble in the Highways Department yard – it took rescuers an hour to extract just ten people. The WVS fed, comforted and clothed them and Civil Defence volunteers, trained by school kitchen staff, prepared lunch for seventy people in the open air, without the use of mains services of any kind. There were no reports of deaths from boiled cabbage.

The live theatre continued to provide a training ground for future stars. Among those appearing in the lower reaches of the Palace Theatre's variety bills in 1954 were Cleo Laine, Shirley Bassey and Ken Dodd. And if you did not want to watch the stars, there was a total eclipse of the sun in 1954. Light cloud meant people could look at it without the usual eye protection. For those who missed it, the paper published the date of the next one – 7 October 2135.

One of the theatrical events of Reading's year was a week's appearance at the Palace by the current teenagers' idol, Dickie Valentine, the 25-year-old former singer with the Ted Heath Band. Hundreds of women queued for autographs, stroked his hair and tore at his clothes. 'He's like a Greek God!' cried one swooning fan. Redina of the Women's Page was less complimentary, describing him as 'medium height, mouse haired, on the podgy side, with features to match'.

On the subject of live spectacles, the circus came to town in a big way. Chipperfield's Circus claimed to be the biggest in Europe, with a big top that could seat 6,000 people and more animals than you would find in the average safari park. They claimed to have sixteen elephants, seventy horses, camels and llamas galore, eighteen bears, lions, performing poodles, sealions, snakes and, of course, George the Giraffe. Many of these (but presumably not the sealions and snakes) took part in a grand parade from the railway station to the circus site at Hills Meadow. Almost lost among this menagerie were the fifty international artistes of the human variety and the mayor, who was present to greet them.

The Women's Page sought ideas from its readers for inventions to make their lives easier. Many of their dreams were to come true – the waste disposal unit for sinks, electrically heated curling tongs and a compact dishwashing machine – but the world is still waiting for the electric pram (for hilly districts) and the special vacuum cleaner for removing ashes from the fire grate. The column also did its level best to perpetuate the myth of women as consumer bimbos:

> Where does a woman make her influence felt most when it comes to buying a car? 'Colour', says the salesman. 'When a man customer has made up his mind about everything else, if there's a woman in the picture anywhere, she is always consulted about the colour. And if there is a choice between black and lighter shades, the lighter shade gets the woman's vote. A woman puts a great deal of thought into deciding what colour car to have,' a Reading garage salesman told me.

They even offered colour hints for the woman car buyer – navy blue cars were considered dowdy, while olive green was the most difficult colour to coordinate with your wardrobe.

Worse violence from 'the Edwardians' was to come. A crowd of some 500 gathered outside the Olympia ballroom as a whole series of fights broke out between teddy boys and servicemen. One of those arrested denied being a teddy boy, telling the court, 'I have a black suit, but I got it for a dinner and dance'.

Mr Eric Strong of Western Road also appeared before the court, charged with assault. His case was that he acted in self-defence, his assailant having rushed at him with fists raised. He put up his hand to protect himself, causing his attacker to turn around and overbalance, suffering injuries in the fall. The only part of the story that did not gel was the fact that this vicious assault on him was carried out by 92-year-old Mrs Florence Witts. Strong was fined £5 and bound over to keep the peace. Equally convincing was a man arrested for exposing himself in the cinema, who pleaded in mitigation the fact that he was deaf. (Presumably he didn't hear the usherette coming.) And in another case a doctor, treating a youth for a case of acne, was alleged to have performed an act of gross indecency with him. According to the prosecuting Counsel, 'The boy is not one of high intelligence, and did not realise that things of this sort were nothing to do with his treatment.'

Although it was not recognised at the time, 1954 saw the beginning of the end of Huntley & Palmer's long association with Reading. They announced the construction of a new factory in Huyton, near Liverpool, to serve the northern markets which had been denied them when zoning was introduced during the war. The factory would employ 800 people, with room for expansion. It would eventually lead to the closure of manufacturing, and later the severing of all business links, with Reading. But if Reading was losing its biscuits, it was gaining coffee. The town's first coffee bar opened:

NEW READING RESTAURANT
FIRST TO PROVIDE 'EXPRESSO' COFFEE
The addition to Reading's cafe facilities of 'expresso', the latest coffee craze from Italy, was greeted enthusiastically by guests at the opening party of 'Palomino' in Duke Street, the first restaurant in town to install one of the glittering machines which produce this kind of coffee.

In a setting which is an attractive blend of South American and contemporary styles Mr J.W. Clough, the proprietor of 'Palomino', introduced his guests to 'cappuccino', the frothing creamy drink so different from the average English

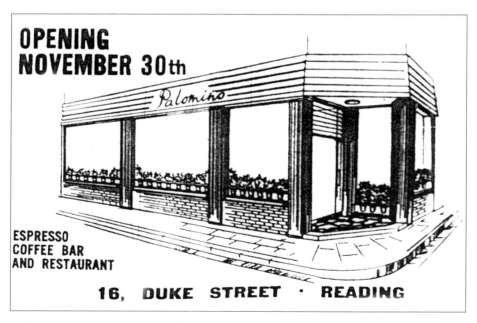

Coffee bar culture comes to Reading.

Santa arrives in his helicopter at McIlroy's.

white coffee. . . . The Editor of the *Berkshire Chronicle* was . . . initiated into the habit which has swept London in the last year and is now steadily spreading into the provinces.

The growth of phone use in Reading led to the need to change the numbers. The four-digit numbers, which were supposed to last the town for thirty years, were all used up in twenty. Complicated plans to move to five-figure numbers were announced, complete with a 'golden-voiced' telephonist, who would tell mis-diallers to look the new number up in the phone book. (The idea of customer care had presumably not yet been invented.) As compensation they promised that, within five years, it would be possible to direct-dial to numbers on automatic exchanges within 25 miles of Reading.

For once, Santa was beaten to it in the rush to announce Christmas as soon as possible after the longest day. The 24 September edition of the *Chronicle* carried an advertisement from Fergusons, the wine merchants, advising customers to stock up early for Christmas (and then presumably drink it all before the event). Nearer the day, the paper foretold what the lucky (or not so lucky) child could expect in his or her Christmas stocking. It included Timex 'Hopalong Cassidy' or 'Cinderella' watches (47s 6d), Little Bo Peep cutlery sets (3s 11d), Muffin the Mule slippers (10s 3d) and Pedigree dolls (79s 6d). But what we really wanted was the Stratoblaster Space Gun (14s 11d).

SIX

1955: Smog and ITV

The new year opened with the news that Santa was dead. Seventy-year-old ex-lorry driver Robert Trown had taken great pleasure in his job as Father Christmas at one of the town's department stores. Not surprisingly, he was told on Christmas Eve that his services were no longer required, and he became very depressed. Six days later, his body was found in a gas-filled room at his home in Coventry Road.

One store that would not have need of a Father Christmas in future years was McIlroys. It was announced in January that the long-established department store was to close, with the loss of 230 jobs. This was done not for lack of trade but to take advantage of a boom in property values – their Oxford Road premises fetched £181,000.

Residents of Bulmershe raised a furore about Reading Borough Council's plans to build council houses on 47 acres in the area. They wanted to see private housing, if the land had to be developed at all. The reason, they told to the press, was that they feared rate rises, despite categorical assurances from Wokingham council officials that this would not be the case. There were calls for a clear Green Belt to be created between Reading and its neighbours. Duncan Sandys, the Minister for Housing and Local Government, obliged shortly afterwards by calling for local authorities nationally to submit plans for Green Belts around their settlements.

The paper was at a loss to know where Reading could draw its boundaries for a Green Belt, given that areas like Bulmershe and Sonning were virtually merged into Reading and there was little scope for inserting a Green Belt anywhere between Bracknell and Reading. They also took the opportunity to bemoan the dead hand of bureaucracy, presumably for getting the area into this situation: 'If only local authorities had some of the vision of individual enterprise, what a different world it would be!'

One of the most unusual homes in Reading disappeared during the year. Since 1946 Mr and Mrs Colombe had lived in an old barge, the *Evelyn Maude*, which stood on a piece of dry land at the Warren, surrounded by flower beds. It had become quite a local landmark and was equipped with mains water, electricity and a telephone. However, it had seen better days and the owners decided to have a bungalow built on the plot. They had to break up the barge, since it blocked their view of the river.

Another family with an original solution to the housing problem were the Petries of Tilehurst. For months they were encamped in two buses on a site in Gypsy Lane, Tilehurst, which was required for development. When all other methods of shifting them failed, they were towed off by a bulldozer to a grass verge on Kentwood Hill. There again, they resisted attempts to move them on, forever promising that they were going next week. Eventually they found themselves hauled up before the court and fined £6.

Another court case ensued when police saw a group of drunks tottering around a car. They identified the owner and advised him that he was not in a fit state to drive. He replied to the officer, 'I am going to drive it. I am a better driver drunk than you are sober.' This was the wrong answer and cost him £10 and a year's ban.

January saw the arrival of Manchester United at Elm Park for an FA Cup third round match. Matt Busby's team included eight internationals, including 'Busby Babes' like Duncan Edwards and Tommy Taylor, both of whom tragically were to die in the Munich air crash of 1958. Despite this star-studded opposition, Reading took an early lead from an own goal and held it until seven minutes from time, when United got an equaliser. The replay at Old Trafford was played in a blizzard, and United won 4–1.

Reading play Manchester United in the FA Cup and a small boy has a day to remember.

The rest of the 1954/55 season was less auspicious, with Reading languishing in the bottom half of the Third Division (South). The habitual excuses about unprecedented injury problems appeared in the paper although, to be fair, they did at one time have no fewer than seven players in plaster. The 1955/56 season started even more disastrously. The manager resigned, suffering from strain and, by the week before Christmas, they were next to bottom of the league.

A new health hazard threatened the people of Reading – especially the elderly – and a new word was coined:

SMOG

Mr J.W. Stewart, the Secretary of the Coal Merchants' Federation, made some interesting observations at the annual dinner of the Berkshire Coal Merchants' Association. In the course of his speech he had something to say about that horrible hybrid newcomer to the English language – 'smog'. What our parents and their forebears knew as 'the London Particular' . . . has long been a source of irritation and discomfort, but it is only in recent times that the medico and the statistician have laid bare the havoc to health and industry of this seasonal visitation. In addition, modern publicity has widely spread the dread intelligence, and one more terror has arrived to harass the elderly as winter comes. The Clean Air Bill has emerged from the mild panic.

Smokeless fuel, which, by the way, is virtually unobtainable when it is most needed – will, it is admitted, do much to relieve air pollution; but the nation is warned that it will be a very long time before there is enough of this commodity to go round.

From there, the editorial went into an extraordinary lament for the imminent passing of the open fire and its replacement by nuclear energy, waxing lyrical along the lines of 'in castle and cottage hearts have been gladdened by the yuletide log'. It then waded into 'the octopus of bureaucracy' which it claimed was snatching liberty from the individual, as if the freedom to poison your neighbours with smoke were a fundamental human right.

Lovers of a smog-free country life will have been heartened by the opening in April of the Museum of English Rural Life at Reading University. The Museum had been in existence for four years behind closed doors, but this was the first chance the public had to look at more than 4,000 exhibits, illustrating every aspect of life in rural England.

One Reading man who was doing very well for himself was the vice-captain of the English touring cricketers in Australia, Peter May. They successfully retained the Ashes in the 1954/55 tour and plans were announced for a civic reception for him on his return. More than 500 people paid 5s a head to meet him and other sporting celebrities. In fact, the test team in 1955 contained two Reading-born players, when 24-year-old Surrey batsman Ken Barrington was selected to play against South Africa at Lords.

Also packing them in, and this time by remote control, was evangelist Billy Graham. His meeting at the Kelvin Hall, Glasgow, was relayed to Reading Town Hall, where 1,400 people overflowed from the main town hall into the small hall. Fifty-eight converts came forward at the end of the meeting. Less successful was the local Communist-turned-evangelist Charles Potter, who held a Billy Graham-style crusade on the same Whitley estate where he had once led a rent protest. After his stirring oration, he invited people to come forward and give themselves to God. No one moved a muscle.

A General Election was called for 26 May. Reading had been reduced from two parliamentary seats to one, and it was to be a straight fight between the two sitting MPs, Ian Mikardo and F.M. Bennett. The Liberals decided not to contest it. As always, heavyweight politicians came to Reading in support of the candidates. Prime Minister Anthony Eden stopped briefly on his way through the town to deliver a rallying call to some 3,000 supporters gathered beneath the balcony of Somerset House, opposite the town hall.

No election campaign involving Ian Mikardo was likely to be dull. This sample from his election address sums him up:

> If you choose me again as your representative, you'll have to put up with a man who tries to think things out for himself and then says what he thinks. If you want an M.P. who always follows his party's line, who never says or does anything unpopular, and who slavishly models himself on his leaders in the hope of getting promotion, I'm not your man and you had better find someone else to vote for.

Prime Minister Anthony Eden draws a big crowd to Town Hall Square.

A row broke out when someone defaced the posters outside Labour campaign headquarters by writing 'Big Brother is watching You' on them and drawing a moustache (Stalinesque, presumably, rather than the Hitler-type) on a picture of Mikardo. This coincided with a visit to the town by Aneurin Bevin (though he was not suspected of the deed). The Labour agent accused Tory supporters of this outrage and Mikardo put up posters next to the amended ones, saying 'Disfigured by Reading Tories'. The Conservative agent frothed with indignation and sought legal advice.

Bevin's visit to Reading was itself not without incident. He was heckled when he claimed that some Tories had connived in the outbreak of the Second World War and Conservative infiltrators to the meeting unfurled a banner saying 'Vote for Eden – You can trust him'. In the event, Mikardo won by the narrowest of margins – 238 votes – after a recount.

But according to Mr R.M. Bradbury, they need not have bothered with an election since the world was about to be destroyed. He told an audience of Jehovah's Witnesses at the town hall that the present order was about to be swept away and replaced by a New World System, under the righteous administration of Jesus.

There were early signs of the office boom that was to transform Reading – for better or worse – in the sixties and beyond. The foundation stone of one of Reading's modern landmarks – the Thames Conservancy building by Reading Bridge – was laid, and the paper praised it as a fine building that led the way. At the same time they bemoaned the state of the rest of Reading's riverside, despite the efforts of the council over several decades to improve it. Plans were also announced for Prudential's new development on the corner of Friar Street and Station Road, which had been delayed since 1939 and which had the approval of no less a body than the Royal Fine Art Commission. The question of Reading's heritage was brought into focus by this new development:

THE HEAVY HAND OF PROGRESS
The impending demolition by an insurance company of what is, perhaps, the finest early eighteenth-century house in Reading – number 16 Friar Street – to make way for a block of offices, has raised the question whether an inventory should not now be made, with interior and exterior photographs, of all, or at least the majority, of the old houses in the town. A surprising number still remain, although many of them have been masked by modern fronts. It is inevitable in the present age, when business is avidly seeking central accommodation, that hands should be laid upon buildings which have passed the peak of their usefulness and remain as tidemarks of a more leisurely day. The desire to preserve the best of them is natural to those who cherish the more attractive architecture of the past, but the fight is invariably an unequal one.

Another piece of Reading's heritage that was under threat was the Kennet & Avon Canal, as a parliamentary bill was proposed that would allow it to be abandoned. This led to the formation of the Reading branch of the Kennet & Avon Canal Association, and to protests mounted by Berkshire County Council and the novelist A.P. Herbert. At this time, the case was still argued in terms

'I must ask you to accompany me to the station – very quickly!' Fun from the Reading Police sports day in 1955.

of its potential for carrying commercial freight, rather than leisure traffic. It was claimed that 100,000 tons of freight (later raised to 200,000 as campaign hysteria built up steam) were waiting to use it. Another argument advanced for it was that, in wartime, it was big enough to carry naval patrol vessels and landing craft.

The extraordinary case came to light of a 51-year-old man who, for more than forty years, had been virtually imprisoned in his house and treated as an invalid by his parents. Charlie Dunford had contracted measles as a seven-year-old and his parents had developed an irrational fear that he would go blind if he were allowed out. He was kept in a darkened room, carried about the house and fed on invalid food. The authorities only found him after the death of his parents and he had to be taught such basics as wearing shoes, walking, speaking and feeding himself.

The health of the economy did not appear to be a problem for the government – it was reported in February that, in the area which covered Reading, there were 185 vacancies for every 100 unemployed people. Staff shortages were more of a problem, and were cited as one of the reasons for Huntley & Palmer's choice of Huyton, near Liverpool, for their new factory. This new, highly automated plant opened during the year and, almost straight away, plans for its expansion were announced. The editorial column assumed, wrongly, that the same principles of automation would be introduced in their Reading premises. Huntley & Palmer ultimately had a more radical solution to the local labour supply problem.

Those who look back with nostalgia to bygone days will be pleased to know that the 1950s even had a nicer class of hooligan. The Chief Constable of Reading, Jesse Lawrence, explained it all to the pupils of Woodley Hill Grammar School at their speech day:

> It may surprise you to know that in dealing with criminals police officers find they very often have a feeling of some admiration for them; a mutual respect exists between men of the criminal class and the police. When I say that, I am not referring to those horrible types who indulge in crimes of violence. And I have no intention of eulogising criminals, whom it is my intention to stamp out if possible. . . .
>
> We hear a lot about teddy boys. People say 'What are you going to do about these teddy boys?' But such boys are not a novelty. They used to be called hobble-de-hoys and afterwards just hooligans. They are only boys who have not had the benefit of a good home, as you have. The only way to deal with them is to ignore them.

Unless, of course, you were an evangelist, in which case your duty was to save them.

'NEW LIFE' FOR TEDDY BOYS
READING CONVERSION CAMPAIGN
A religious revival campaign, which has led to the conversion of a number of 'teddy' boys and girls – or, as they call themselves, 'yobboes' – is being conducted

by a group of lay evangelists in Reading. . . . One of the chief assistants is an ex-teddy boy Donald Mundy, who was converted to the Christian faith last year and is now anxious to become a missionary. Every Saturday evening the group, with their new converts, hold open air meetings in St Mary's Butts and the Town Hall Square, Reading, and attract large crowds. Then Donald Mundy, dressed in his full Edwardian suit, proudly witnesses to his conversion and the new life he has found.

Mr and Mrs James Burnett, of Wokingham Road, were the evangelists responsible for this remarkable transformation. After a long discussion with them, the teddy boys accepted a challenge to attend an evangelistic evening: 'We had a grand Christian social evening, including a chorus-singing session to the accompaniment of a piano-accordian, ukelele, banjo and tambourine. From that night on, they have been getting converted and coming to my home every night.' None of that 'I sold my soul for rock and roll' in the 1950s.

Commercial television made its appearance in 1955. Advertisers, or 'sponsors' as they preferred to call them, were to pay the fabulous sum of £1,000 per minute at weekend peak hours. The attractions for the viewer included *Double your Money* with Hughie Green and the two American series *Dragnet* and *I Love Lucy*. For the children, there was Roy Rogers, and Richard Greene starred as Robin Hood. Sunday nights were spent at the London Palladium in the company of Tommy Trinder. But not all their first shows passed into television's hall of fame. Whatever became of the panel game *It's an Idea* or *Pet's Parade*? The BBC had their own secret weapon against the competition. They televised the silver wedding celebrations of Wilfred and Mabel Pickles.

Response to the new channel was mixed. Some claimed the reception on the new channel was better than the BBC – less affected by trolley buses – and that the programmes were much slicker and brighter than the staid BBC. Others reported switching back to BBC, infuriated with the advertisements. What was clear was that the television age had arrived; this was the first year in which television viewing outstripped audiences for the radio.

It was also the motor age. Everybody seemed to want a car and the paper was concerned about it:

How our already grossly overcrowded roads are going to cope with it all is hard to imagine; that the face of Britain and certain aspects of the life of its people, especially in the cities and the towns, will have to change within a comparatively few years from now is, however, certain.

The British Road Federation had their solution worked out:

A start should be made by 1958 on building the first stretch of Britain's first motorway linking London with Yorkshire. When it is finished, traffic outside built-up areas will be speeded up with safety. But traffic in cities will still be condemned to crawl, wasting millions in lost time, needlessly high fuel consumption and engine wear, not to mention frayed nerves.

The coming of commercial television prompted a new flood of TV owners.

Motorways must therefore be carried through heavily built-up urban areas to ease congestion in narrow old streets and thus cut road costs which are reflected in the cost of living.

Their vision continued with a nightmare picture of flyovers and elevated streets, carving their way through the centre of our towns and cities in the name of reduced engine wear.

Far from supporting the unbridled freedom of traffic, there were calls for heavy vehicles to be banned from using Reading town centre, because of the congestion they were causing in St Mary's Butts. It was suggested that there should be a time limit on the hours of deliveries (an idea picked up much more recently in the town's pedestrianisation) to enable the buses to move more freely. The Chamber of Commerce wanted the town to have some of the new-fangled parking meters, like they used in Canada. The only problem was that there were no legal powers to allow the council to install them.

A novel new bus was also on trial in Reading at that time – it weighed 30 hundredweight less than a conventional bus, carried 61 passengers against the normal 52 and, strangest of all, had its engine in the back, rather than in

The BMW Isetta – from the days before the company went up-market.

Great Western Motors promote the new bubble cars. Draping the model over the bonnet was not an option.

the proper place. The railways suffered from a lengthy strike, starting at the Whitsun bank holiday weekend. Some local industry was badly hit – the Pulsometer factory claimed to have goods piling up and elsewhere there were threats of factory layoffs – and horse racing in the London area was banned for the duration of the strike.

For the aspiring car owner, these were the days of the affordable BMW. The Isetta model boasted seating for two adults and a small child, a 245cc engine that gave a top speed of 55mph and 87mpg, and a one-door model was the only option. This may help to explain why yuppies were not invented until the 1980s.

Somebody who would not be driving for a while was Mr Albert Walker. He was so incensed when his son failed his driving test that he tried to run down the examiner. With the same impeccable driving skill that he had obviously passed on to his son, he missed. But he got close enough to earn himself a £10 fine and a six-month ban.

The Queen Mother came to Reading to open the new Technical College (rumoured controversially to have cost £1 million). As part of her visit she called in on Huntley & Palmers, where she saw a replica of her own wedding cake and met sixteen-year-old Colin Golding. She asked him how long he had been at his

The Queen Mother meets a Huntley & Palmer employee encased in a tank. Did he forget to press his trousers for the royal visit?

job (dough rolling) and whether he liked it. For some reason, the paper failed to record Mr Golding's replies. We were, however, told by Mr Golding how it felt to be spoken to by the Queen Mother; apparently it gave him an awfully funny feeling inside.

One of the best-kept secrets of the year was the Civil Defence recruitment drive, held one Sunday in October. Just as the families of Reading were settling down to their Sunday lunches at home, the Civil Defence volunteers prepared to serve up lunch for 150 people to an almost non-existent crowd. At least the mayor was there, stoically working his way through a meal eaten with a blue plastic spoon. Also present were the Casualties Union, adding realism to the exercise with heart-rending screams of simulated agony. Unfortunately, the first aid tent had been located next to the communications centre, and the screams played havoc with the radio messages.

It was the first Christmas of the television ratings battle. The BBC had Beniamino Gigli (the Pavarotti of his day) plus some more lowbrow crooners including Alma Cogan, Ruby Murray and Jimmy Young, the latter in the days before he became better known as a disc jockey. The commercial channel fought back with Norman Wisdom in *Cinderella*. The glow of the yuletide log had been replaced by that of the cathode ray tube. At least it did not cause smog.

SEVEN

1956: Rock Around the Clock

New year 1956 started quietly, unless you were at a private party. New Year's Eve being on a Sunday, all places of public entertainment were forced by their licences to close by 11.45 p.m. However, the Heelas Social Club had taken over the Great Western Hotel and it was therefore allowed to see in the new year. Meanwhile, down at the fire station on Caversham Road, carousing firemen welcomed 1956 by releasing balloons and ringing the bells of their fire appliances, no doubt to the great joy of any neighbours trying to sleep.

Reading shoppers, ready to kill for a bargain in the January sales.

There was more evidence of the power of the new medium of television. Over Christmas, they had shown a preview of the Walt Disney film *Davy Crockett*. Now, the theme music was forever on the radio and the consumer craze that had swept America looked set to conquer Reading, as the stores stocked up with coonskin caps and flintlock cap pistols. The Women's Page reported the first sighting of a miniature frontiersman on the streets in much the same way as the first cuckoo of spring. It was reported that the Davy Crockett hats were made of 'real fur fabric', leading the Women's Page to speculate as to what 'imitation fur fabric' was like.

There were signs that the days of the trolley buses in Reading were numbered. When proposals came up in council to extend the network of routes, they were opposed in some quarters on the grounds that trolley buses were costly and inflexible. Diesel and petrol were said to be the motive power for the buses of the future, and a recent example was cited of a trolley bus which brought the town centre to a standstill when its aerial pole got caught up in the overhead wires. The supporters of the trolley buses replied that they were quieter, more comfortable and less polluting – and they survived, for the time being.

Another 'obsolete' form of transport was also gathering support. Opponents of the closure of the Kennet & Avon Canal were gathering a petition while paddling its length in a canoe. This was the only craft that could navigate the derelict waterway and, even then, it had to be carried for about 2 miles of its overgrown length. By the time they reached Reading, the petition already had some 21,000 signatures and a crowd of supporters gathered at High Bridge to add their names to it. The petition was destined for Westminster Pier and the Houses of Parliament. They were successful – a clause added to the Transport Commission Bill reprieved the canal. A fleet of cruisers tried to celebrate by navigating the canal from Reading to Theale, but were unable to get any further than Burghfield Lock. Later in the year, the chairman of the council's Health Committee claimed that the stagnant waters of the Kennet & Avon were a breeding ground for mosquito infestations and a potential health hazard.

A famous waterside landmark was disappearing from Reading. For 300 years the Freebody family had built boats at their site next to Caversham bridge. Now, 72-year-old Mrs Rose Freebody announced the imminent closure of the firm. Also known as 'the grand old lady of the Thames' (a soubriquet which suggests a barge, rather than a white-haired grandmother), Mrs Freebody offered the firm's 400 yard frontage at a bargain price to the Borough Council if they would build a lido there, but the council declined the offer. Freebody's had themselves provided a lido, complete with 32 foot diving board, until its closure a couple of years before. Undeterred, Mrs Freebody set out to try to attract private sector funding. Today, the site is occupied by flats.

Another local institution was celebrating 150 years in the town – a relative newcomer in Freebody's terms. Suttons seed company had begun life in 1806 as a small shop in Market Place. By 1956 they employed 700 staff, had 5 acres of offices and warehouses and 150 acres of trial grounds. Their days in Reading were also relatively numbered. By 1974, they were to announce their departure from Reading to Torquay – another victim of Reading's labour shortages.

The Women's Page continued to offer up its unique insights into life. One week it dispelled the notion that folk dancing was only for long-haired intellectuals (assuming that anyone had ever held such an idea). The next, it told readers about a knitting pattern for a smog cap, a garment like a balaclava but which left only the eyes exposed – ideal for preventing the inhalation of smog (or for folk dancers who wanted to disguise the fact that they were long-haired intellectuals).

Rivalry between the television networks was hotting up. It was reported that ITV spent the fabulous sum of £70,000 on their main Easter attraction, the *Bob Hope Show*. A large part of that must have gone to pay Hope's total of no fewer than five joke writers. There were fears that this kind of extravaganza would make audiences discontented with home-grown products. Again the BBC responded, announcing that their coverage of Wimbledon this year would involve the use of no fewer than four cameras. Viewers would not only be able to see Centre and Number One courts, they would also have a panoramic view of the outside courts.

A local showbusiness connection was re-established when popular songstress Alma Cogan revisited her childhood home – the tailor's shop of Mr A. Kogan in Kings Road. It was her first visit in ten years and it took her an hour to sign autographs for the waiting crowd.

The safety of the new privately owned atomic reactor at Aldermaston was still a matter of public concern. The supervising engineer, Mr J.N. Barnett, told the local parish council: 'It is not a bomb but an inherently safe device even if the safety precautions fail.' The local Medical Officer of Health supported his views. Their faith was tested later in the year, when the centre was threatened by a major forest fire which, at its peak, covered some 25 acres. Many fire brigades, including the USAAF force from Greenham Common, were called out to bring the fire under control, as people were evacuated from the site as a precaution.

Atomic Weapons Establishments were, however, considered to be injurious to education. The Chairman of Berkshire Education Committee reported that they attracted more families with children to the area, while at the same time drawing building labour away from essential school construction. Hospital technicians, too, were in short supply locally, as they were attracted to Aldermaston by the better pay and conditions on offer there.

The Workers' Education Association was looking to the future – to a time when automation would bring a 30- to 35-hour week, more holidays and earlier retirement. However, Mr Charles Ford of the AEU Research Department was able to tell them that few jobs would be amenable to automation – certainly not more than 10 per cent of the workforce. He did, however, predict that:

Another example of automation was the electronic device for calculating such things as payrolls and doing ledger and other clerical work. This would bring about major advances and drastic changes in banking and insurance.

Thus Reading received its first warning of the arrival of the computer age. There was change, too, on the fashion front:

MEN'S FASHION DUE FOR CHANGE
Beware, you elegant men-about-town! As far as I can see, you are about to lose one of your favourite weekend uniforms – the duffle coat and suede shoes. Why? Because the young lads and teenagers who throng Reading's streets every

Saturday are taking up these two items in a big way and experience shows that, when that happens, the initiators of the fashion lose interest in it and think up something else.

The Women's Page speculated as to what the next male fashion trend might be and, with wild inaccuracy, came up with a revival of the smoking jacket under the guise of the television jacket, along with matching boxer shorts and jackets for the beach.

Equal opportunities were raising their head as a matter of public concern. There was a heated debate about equal pay for women teachers at the Berkshire Education Committee. Arguments about dignity, equal standing and discrimination were dismissed by the likes of Cllr Mrs Jarvis, who argued, along with the majority, that: 'We have been able to go a long way in education in this county simply because we have not brought forward extravagant schemes to the council.' Equality for black people (then referred to as 'coloured', as if the other kind were transparent) was also the subject of media interest:

RACIAL ANTAGONISM: NOT WIDESPREAD IN READING

'My impression of Reading is that racial antagonism is not so widespread as in some other towns I have visited', writes Roy McFarlane in the new journal for coloured folk, *Our Sphere*.

He adds: 'The shopkeepers and publicans never refuse to serve coloured people. The bus conductors are rather courteous and helpful to the stranger. . . . I wish more employers would be prepared to offer employment to coloured people on their merits, rather than on racial considerations. And white landlords and landladies could greatly help to solve our housing problems by coming forward with offers of accommodation.'

Office life, before the days of the photocopier, fax and PC.

According to their calculations, some 250 West Indians lived in Reading at that time. The number had grown from virtually none a few years before and was expected to double by 1957. For entertainment, most of them went to the International Club: 'The atmosphere of this club is rather friendly, very unlike the dancehalls where the whites refuse to mix with the coloureds.'

There were serious problems in the cinemas. Seat slashing (costing £4 a time to repair) was widespread and one manager said the Teddy Girls were the worst culprits. The film *Rock around the Clock* was banned across Berkshire by an emergency meeting of the County Council. They were told: 'As this film has proved to be an excuse for hooliganism in other towns in the country, the Chief Constable considered that it was in the public interest that this film should be banned in this county.' After an article referring to the problems being caused by teddy boys and girls generally in local cinemas, the paper's editor was threatened with an acid bomb attack if he printed one more word about teddy boys.

It was in this context that the editorial column lent its support both to the banning of the film, and to a campaign led by the Vice-Chancellor of Reading University, Sir John Wolfenden, to raise funds for the National Federation of Mixed Clubs and Girls' Clubs.

> The risk could not be taken of disorder on the scale that has ensued in other places where the film has been shown.
>
> But it is important that the public, not less than the teddy boys and girls, should not lose its sense of proportion. 'There is nothing alarming in rock and roll' said Dr J. Macalister Brew, Director of Education to the National Association of Mixed Clubs and Girls' Clubs.
>
> With certain reservations, we are inclined to agree with him. It is the contagion of enthusiasm which leads the mild addict into the arena of disorder. . . . If the frenzy of rock and roll has nourished youthful mass hysteria till it has found vent at times in dangerous manifestations, how much is due to the lack of any other vent for adolescent energy? Some of the answer may be the Mixed Clubs, for which Sir John Wolfenden pleaded so eloquently at a meeting this week 'where boys and girls might learn how to behave towards each other, find their common interests and develop and grow as citizens of tomorrow'.

The paper also bemoaned the lack of spiritual guidance for young people at social clubs: 'The purely secular approach is too likely to leave the young man or woman exposed, without spiritual protection, to the temptations of the world.'

One person who clearly suffered from a severe lack of spiritual protection was the self-styled 'King of the Teddy Boys', 'Mad Charlie' – or, as the courts preferred to describe him, 25-year-old storeman Desmond Turrell of Orts Road. Turrell appeared before the court charged with assault and actual bodily harm. It was the latest addition to a remarkable criminal record going back some twenty-one years and encompassing pre-school bicycle theft, unlawful possession of firearms, an army court martial for theft and firearms offences, borstal for driving a car without consent, escape from borstal, numerous housebreakings and other offences, an indecent act and an assault on the police. One of the few things he could not be accused of was cinema seat slashing, since he was already banned from most of the town's places of entertainment. He asked the court to give him a chance and not send him to prison – which, surprisingly, they did, fining him £30, to be paid off at £1 a week.

Their faith was not rewarded. Within a matter of weeks, he was up before the High Wycombe magistrates, this time on a charge of assaulting a police inspector while visiting that town to see *Rock Around the Clock* at one of the few cinemas where neither he nor the film was banned. Once again, he sought leniency from the court, telling them that he had a steady job and a steady girlfriend for the first time. This time, the magistrates were having none of it, and sent him to prison for six months. By the time he was due for release, Berkshire County Council had relented on its ban on *Rock around the Clock*, and had also certificated another controversial item, the so-called 'sunbathing film' *Garden of Eden*.

The Duke of Edinburgh was doing his bit to prevent people's youths being misspent. He announced the launch of an award scheme bearing his name for boys aged between fifteen and eighteen. It covered first aid and rescue work, 'venturesome causes' and physical fitness. If the trial scheme were successful, it was planned to extend it into a range of schools and voluntary organisations.

At the other end of the moral spectrum, a Reading clergyman was doing his level best to help schoolboys misspend their time. He was hauled up before the Bow Street magistrates and fined £5 for attempting to importune boys at the Schoolboys Own Exhibition at Westminster. He apologised to the court and promised never to come to London alone again, to give up drinking entirely, and never to enter a public lavatory unless absolutely obliged.

Also up before the court was a 58-year-old company director, who had started his day's marathon drinking rather too early. He confessed to having consumed his regular daily diet of one and a half bottles of whisky before lunch on the day of the arrest. The vigilant officers attending the scene detected a hint of alcohol on his breath. He was charged with being drunk in charge of a vehicle. His defence – that he was not in charge of the vehicle in the sense that he was so drunk that he was physically incapable of getting into it and driving – did not greatly impress the magistrates. Drivers like him were the target of the Reading Temperance Society, who launched a call for compulsory blood tests for those suspected of driving under the influence. In his case, it would be more a matter of finding traces of blood in his alcohol stream.

Drink was also the downfall of Henry Hensley of Henley Road, Caversham, who was somewhat surprised to wake up on his wedding morning in a police cell, with no recollection of how he got there. The court was able to refresh his memory. He had been found lying on the pavement by a police officer, considerably the worse for wear. While being helped to his feet he had attempted to assault the officer. He was fined £5 and despatched without delay to his second pressing engagement of the morning.

Road safety was on the mind of another Reading man:

SAFETY FOR MOTORISTS
READING MAN'S INVENTION
Every month we hear of the mounting toll of victims in road accidents. So far this year, over thirty deaths have been recorded on Berkshire's roads. . . . Ways are constantly being sought to keep these accident figures down, but few are so simple and so inexpensive as the one advocated by Mr J.R. Sturge-Whiting of 7A West Street, Reading.

He has invented a car safety belt, which would cut down the extent of injuries to motorists and passengers when involved in a smash. 'In most cases when there is a severe crash the front seat passenger comes off worst by being thrown forward,' says Mr Sturge-Whiting. 'My safety belt would prevent that.'

The article went on to explain why his design, which was based on aircraft technology, was better than all previous such proposals. We learned also that Mr Sturge-Whiting had a personal interest in the campaign. His brother-in-law had recently been killed in a car accident and a seat belt might have saved him.

An unusual traffic hazard was worrying the parents of pupils at E.P. Collier School – cattle. They held a meeting to complain that their children could not walk to school safely for the number of cattle being moved through the streets of the town. They allegedly terrified the children, held up the traffic, damaged adjoining gardens and polluted the air and the streets, as they made their way from the railway sidings to a field in Caversham where they were kept temporarily. Bang on cue, just as Ian Mikardo got involved, about a hundred head of cattle got out of control and ran amok in the residential streets near the river. It took their herdsmen about an hour to round them up.

The old McIlroy's store on Oxford Road found a new occupier – one of the first of a new breed of supermarket, yet another American import. The reports spoke highly of it:

> This gleaming contemporary store, with its huge plate-glass windows, yards of refrigerated display and stacks of brightly coloured groceries, brings new convenience and ease to household buying. . . . The supermarket is not merely a new kind of grocery. It aims to cut out numbers of trips to separate shops and provide under one roof the widest possible variety of goods. Here there is a long counter of fresh vegetables and fruit, the vegetables washed and everything prepacked in transparent paper with the price and weight already marked. . . . The shopper will have a wheeled double-decker basket to push around the store. Seven checkouts will cut down waste of time in paying for goods and wrapping them. . . . In addition, there will be something you will probably be surprised to see – nylons. Yes, nylon stockings and at astonishingly low price and high quality. These always sell very well at American supermarkets.

The article went on to describe many of the features familiar to us from modern supermarkets and one that is not – an infra-red grill, where you could choose your chicken and have it cooked in twenty minutes while you completed the rest of your shopping. Other pre-packed food fads from America were reported in the Women's Page that week – pre-packed steaks, one large and one small, labelled 'his' and 'hers', and pre-packed convenience meals, such as mixed grill and tripe and onions.

Such home comforts would be denied the men of the Royal Berkshire Regiment, who were being flown out to 'an unknown destination in the Mediterranean area' as the Suez Crisis worsened. Many of those being called up were reservists, who had been on a seven-year contract – three years in the front line and four in the reserves. Among the unluckiest of these must have been Private Dennis Gearing of Kingsbridge Road, who was demobbed on a Saturday and arrived home to find a telegram waiting for him, calling him up again from the reserves. It was calculated that he had been a civilian for about fifteen minutes.

Reading's Hi-Fi Skiffle Group get to play on BBC Radio's Skiffle Club.

No sooner had the people of Reading got used to the idea of rock and roll than a new musical craze hit the streets. University students were reported doing a charity pub crawl playing something called 'skiffle'. The paper felt it necessary to explain the term:

> What is 'skiffle'? It is the latest jazz rival to rock and roll; a rhythmic melody with words, generally old folk songs or ditties from America's deep south. Instruments are simple. A skiffle group wants only a banjo, a guitar, a double bass and a plain household washboard.

The Suez Crisis deepened, as Britain invaded Egypt in the face of United Nations opposition. Mikardo talked about the moral foundations of the nation's foreign policy being knocked from underneath it. 'Our hands are covered in blood and our heads are covered in shame', he said. He went on to liken the British Government's action to that of Germany in 1914 and 1939. Interestingly, his party leader, Hugh Gaitskell, drew a similar comparison between Hitler and Mussolini and Britain's opponent, Colonel Nasser. Among other things, the closure of the Suez Canal led to the reintroduction of petrol rationing in December. Not everybody saw this as bad news – the papers were full of advertisements for bubble cars, mopeds, electric vans and other fuel-efficient forms of transport.

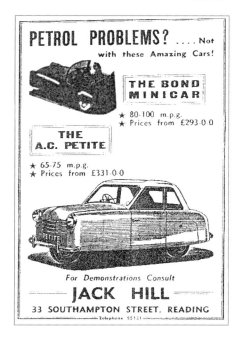

Bubble cars and minicars were very popular, especially when the Suez Crisis led to petrol rationing.

Just as Japan was preparing for another invasion, this time of Britain by its motorcycle industry, the paper forecast a new golden age for British motorcycle manufacturers:

> When the history of the motorcycle movement is written up in years to come, the 1956 Cycle and Motorcycle Show may well be seen as a big turning point in the fashions and images of motorcycling. . . . Machines now being built in British factories have now reached a standard of design and efficiency which places them on an altogether new high level.

The real future of the British motorcycle industry was rather to be seen in their unfortunate attempts to copy the stylish new breed of continental scooters.

Another crisis was taking place in Hungary, as the Russians invaded. An appeal was launched for clothing and money for the refugees. The secretary of the Reading branch of the Save the Children Fund must have been somewhat taken aback by the level of response, having volunteered his own house as a sorting station for the donated clothing. One and a half tons arrived in the first week and, at its height, virtually every room was piled floor to ceiling and teams of twenty to thirty volunteers were busily working their way through it. The first Hungarian refugees arrived in Reading in December, staying at Maiden Erleigh, the former home of millionaire Sol Joel. Christmas Eve also saw the arrival in

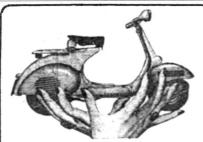

The stylish Italian scooters like the Vespa became a popular form of transport. British attempts to copy them were less successful.

A new housing estate springs up in Tilehurst.

Reading of some 200 refugees – Cypriots, Maltese and others – expelled by Nasser from Egypt.

The Radio Show at Earls Court revealed new technological wonders, such as the interference-free VHF waveband and the transistor. (The paper felt it necessary to explain what a transistor was, in terms of a comparison with a valve.) There were larger than ever televisions on show – some with up to 21-inch screens, battery-powered record players and hi-fi loudspeakers containing two or three units with a crossover filter for much clearer and more realistic reproduction. The latest car radios boasted pre-set stations and also on display were an electronic speech-synthesising machine, an electronic dart board and ERNIE, the computer that picked the winning Premium Bond numbers in the days before we all became hopeless addicts of the National Lottery.

Ian Mikardo MP kept himself constantly in the public eye. He organised a Tribune Brains Trust in Reading, with a panel including Michael Foot. They advocated a reduction in armaments spending of £500 million and an end to conscription by 1957/58. The press envisaged an apocalyptic series of events that would follow from this, with a united Germany becoming a puppet state of Russia and World War III within ten to fifteen years unless the West submitted abjectly to Russia.

Later in the year, Mikardo was in Russia and China, sending back praise of their achievements in education and town planning. The paper expressed the wish that he would stay there and study these wonders in much greater depth. But his finest hour of the year was undoubtedly his speech in Parliament on the Rabbits Bill which, among other things, would give the police powers to arrest wild rabbits being illegally transported. Even the editorial column appreciated his devastating humour in the Commons on this occasion.

Premium Bonds – a favourite flutter in the days before the National Lottery.

State-of-the-art photography, 1950s style.

Father Christmas appeared in the paper, so that meant it must be October. This year, Heelas did not seem to have their heart in it. Their offer to whisk you up to see Santa in the magic lift from the hardware department hardly seemed guaranteed to set tiny pulses racing, despite their claim that 'you can feel the excitement in the air as Christmas comes once again to Heelas'. Wellsteed's Christmas Circus, complete with clowns, jugglers and elephants, sounded much more fun.

EIGHT

1957: Space, and Room to Live

The new year opened with a strike by local electricity workers. Rather unusually, it was prompted by the sacking of a man who had proposed ways of improving efficiency in a department where many staff had been made redundant. New connections and repairs had to be cancelled and there were threats of power cuts if the strike continued for too long.

Another potential strike leader was also in trouble. Ian Mikardo alleged that MI5 was tapping his phone, because he was regarded as a likely cause of industrial strife . 'We are fast on the way to 1984', he warned his audience. But it was not just Mikardo's political enemies who were out to spy on him. His party colleague Ernest Bevin had previously tapped his phone during the Palestinian troubles, since Mikardo had also been an active Zionist. What was of more concern to the paper was Mikardo's further allegation that staff at the university were being called upon to identify potential troublemakers among their numbers to the authorities. This was generally held to be a gross infringement of academic freedom.

Drunkenness in Reading had reached record levels, and there had been a parallel rise in associated offences, such as assaults on police officers. According to police records, 41 per cent of those convicted were of Irish origin. At this time, crimes were often reported in racial or nationalist terms, with headlines like 'West Indian remanded' or 'Polish bricklayer charged with assault'. But the police were ready to deal with any crime wave the Irish, or anyone else, might throw at them. The latest recruits to the force were said to be the absolute cream, and were pictured on the front cover of the paper, resplendent in their blue uniforms and gleaming constabulary badges. According to the paper:

> No recruits to the force have ever passed out of their training with so much confidence. Superbly fit and with their senses razor sharp . . . [they] have only one thing on their minds – crime prevention.

There was only one drawback – they might have some difficulty driving the police car, since they consisted of four Alsatians and a Labrador, the first police dogs to be trained by the Berkshire Constabulary. One of their number, Rex, made his first collar, so to speak, in May, recovering a stolen watch and money from the room of a guilty party at Wellington College.

Evidence of Reading's continuing housing need was given at a public inquiry into a compulsory purchase order for housing land. The inquiry was told that Reading needed to build 6,685 houses over the next ten years, and part of its plans included the housing land at the junction of Bath Road and Burghfield Road. The owner of the land accused the council of breaching the tenth commandment (the one about coveting your neighbour's ox, ass or – though the Bible does not mention it by name – housing land). He wanted to build private – not council – housing on it. But it was revealed to the inquiry that he was fully aware of the council's plans for the land when he bought it.

Another piece of land that was causing a problem was one at Bug's Bottom, where cattle were being stored while in transit for Europe. We heard in the last chapter of the problems they caused while being herded from Reading station to the site. Early in 1957, details of the full scale of the operation became clear. In just six months, 28,000 head of cattle had passed through Reading, in a business worth £1 million a month. Now a new row had broken out, concerning the animals' treatment once they were overseas. Ian Mikardo raised it in Parliament with the Minister, who promised to stop the trade if he received any evidence of ill-treatment.

The cattle trade ended in March, but the residents of Hemdean Road, who had threatened to withhold their rates because of the nuisance the cattle had caused, were still not pleased. Hot on the heels of the cattle came a planning appeal from a local housebuilder to cover 21 acres of Bug's Bottom with development. The developer claimed the land would stand idle if it were not built upon. The council, for its part, said there was no need for the extra housing. Land to build homes for 20–25,000 people had already been earmarked on the fringes of Reading. On this occasion, at least, the minister of the day heeded the council's case.

Certainly, there was no shortage of suggestions about where to put any extra housing. Local builder W.F. Wise was busy arguing that Reading's overspill must go out to the surrounding villages where, as it happened, he was seeking planning permission for some housebuilding.

One alternative to going out was going up, and the council announced ambitious plans to build fifteen-storey blocks of flats on the Coley Park estate. There was also talk of expanding the new town at Bracknell from 25,000 to 40,000 people, sparking fears of a continuous belt of development from Tilehurst to Ascot. Finally, in Earley and Woodley, proposals were published that would almost double the parishes' population from 18,000 to 32,000. The paper seemed to be more interested in some wider issues raised by this last scheme:

> It has many doubtful qualities but certain things stand out. First of all, there will be no influx of overspill from London, as in the new town of Bracknell. The plan merely caters for natural growth, redistribution and redevelopment in the area.

At present, the boundaries of the parishes and the status of local authority are not to be disturbed. But can that last? It is obvious that, in the end, the area concerned must become an urban enclave within the jurisdiction of the Berkshire County Council, with delegated powers.

The paper saw the scheme as the only alternative to expanding Reading's boundaries – creating a self-contained community, rather than one relying upon its 'big brother' to the west.

One family in immediate need of a house were Mr and Mrs Dandridge and their four children from Whitley. While they went away for the weekend, the council evicted them, leaving their furniture under a tarpaulin in the front garden and their dog in police custody (no doubt being questioned by the new police dogs). Their crime was not rent arrears or nuisance, but the fact that they had been illegal sub-tenants in a council house. They were forced to sleep, first in their very small van, then in a tent in somebody's back garden (until it blew down in a gale) and finally in Mrs Dandridge's mother's two-bedroomed house. Throughout this progress, they conducted a war of words in the paper with the council, whom they accused of giving preference to foreigners in allocating council houses.

An eighteen-year-old inmate of Reading Prison died. Thomas O'Brian was found in his cell one morning, asphyxiated. He was described as being a minor epileptic and was regularly sedated by the prison authorities. The prison doctor concluded that he had probably had an epileptic fit and suffocated. O'Brian's father wanted to know why, with his medical record, his son was not routinely checked at night. The inquest did not appear interested in this line of inquiry, and returned a verdict of death by misadventure.

Also behind bars was a thirty-year-old bricklayer from Woodley, David Carter. He had strangled his wife, the mother of his three children aged between one and five, because he suspected she was having an affair with a neighbour. Love of animals was at the heart of another matrimonial dispute. Henry Warwick of Ashmore Road loved animals so much that he spent all the rent money on the horses and the dogs. When his wife told him she was leaving him because of his gambling, he said he would kill her first. True to his word, later that night he took an axe to her, putting her in hospital where she needed thirty stitches. His defence was less than convincing:

> I didn't know I used anything. I thought I only hit her with my fist . . . We went to bed and the next thing I can remember is my son shouting at me. I saw my wife was covered in blood and she told me to get out and get an ambulance. . . . I had no intention of hurting her.

What the result would have been if he had meant to hurt her hardly bears thinking about. He was given two years for grievous bodily harm, and could perhaps count himself lucky. The same week, another defendent got four years just for stealing a raincoat and some other items.

The mention of prison bars immediately brings to mind the king of the local teddy boys, 'Mad Charlie' Turrell, who rose to notoriety in the previous chapter. He appeared in the paper in an unfamiliar setting, leading a group of some thirty teddy boys and girls who were presenting a clock to the retiring manager of the Odeon cinema. 'He has always given us a square deal', Charlie told the waiting press. Fears among his admirers that Charlie was going soft were soon dispelled, after a visit to the Rex Cinema, where a ban on him had only recently been lifted. After he was told off by an usherette for causing a disturbance, he warned her 'Your face and figure won't look so good by the time I've finished with you.' When he appeared before the court, charged with threatening behaviour, Chief Inspector Woodford said, 'He is also known as "Mad Charlie". I don't know if he really is mad.' His probation officer said that Turrell 'had exhibitionist tendencies that got out of hand . . . the trouble is he's not fully grown up yet'. Turrell replied that he resented these remarks, though he wisely refrained from speculating about the future state of the probation officer's face or figure.

One Reading cinema manager who could handle trouble was James Dixon. When one of his teenage customers punched him in the face he picked him up, plonked him on a settee and sat on him until the police came. The fact that he weighed sixteen stones made this a remarkably efficient form of restraint. The assailant, Reginald Kurton, survived to pay a fine of £5 with £4 6s costs.

The university was growing apace. From 700 full-time students in 1939, numbers had risen to 1,200 and there were plans to increase this further, to 2,000 by the mid-1960s. The first of the major new buildings on the campus – the Faculty of Letters – was to be opened by the Queen and Prince Philip, along with the Home Secretary, R.A. Butler. The town – and the papers – were abuzz for weeks with the details of the royal couple's first visit to Reading. The royal party would make its way to the town hall, where they would sign a visitors' book on an outdoor dais. They would then drive through the town to the campus. Lamp-posts along the route were painted, in case the queen stopped to check them, and the services of 15,000 patriotic schoolchildren were secured to line the route.

At the university, the members of the royal party were presented with an Establishment Book of the Royal Household of 1727, some speeches were made, some hands shaken and some royal questions asked of the waiting dignitaries (the only one attributed to Prince Philip in the paper was 'Is there a bar in here?'). After some honorary degrees had been distributed, the building was duly opened. The road taken by the royal party through the campus was renamed The Queen's Drive. It turned out there was no bar in the building, so it could not be renamed Phil's Place.

Also visiting the town in the same week was Bertram Mills Circus. Their star turn was Kam, claimed to be the only elephant in the world that could drive a jeep. They could well have been right. What's more, he could probably have taught the police dogs a useful trick or two.

While Kam may not have suffered from the petrol shortage caused by the Suez Crisis, another of Reading's major events was threatened by it. First, lorries became unavailable to pull the floats in Reading University's rag parade, then alternative plans to use a traction engine had to be abandoned owing to insurance problems. The students were preparing for the mammoth task of

Reading turns out for the royal visit.

Miss Reading (right) and Kam the elephant. One of the prizes given to the various Miss Readings over the years was free driving lessons . . . surely not?

pulling them by hand, when somebody came up with the 40 or so gallons of petrol needed by the lorries. The floats anticipated the golden age of satire which was to come in the sixties – but only in a very modest way. Topical jokes about rock and roll, petrol shortages and 'depresso' coffee bars featured alongside the usual subject matter of student humour. One poster which was to be seen everywhere showed the kiss curl of rock star Bill Haley and the slogan 'Don't mock the lock' (a reference which will probably be totally lost on anyone who did not live through the fifties).

The royal name was taken in vain, as another American fashion hit Reading. The first Wimpy Bar opened in West Street. The paper felt a word of explanation was in order:

> What is a Wimpy?
> A pure beef hamburger that has the reputation of being a meal in itself. It has found favour in London's West End – and in Buckingham Palace. The Queen offered Wimpys to her guests at an important reception recently.

Could Wimpys claim a 'By Royal Appointment' coat of arms to go above their doors on the strength of this? Certainly, Wimpys all round at a royal banquet would not have put a strain on the Privy purse – they retailed in Reading at just 1*s* 3*d* each.

Despite the council using £50,000 of its reserves to cushion the increase, the rates went through the roof, up 4s to 19s. Some tried to blame it on the partial de-rating of shop premises, though others queried this. The paper liked to blame it on the profligacy of the council, citing the fact that their spending was up by 84 per cent overall since 1950. They quoted education spending (up 148 per cent in that same period), Museums and Art Galleries (92 per cent) and libraries (80 per cent).

When it came to suggesting where economies could be made, the paper was less forthcoming, accepting that most of what the council did was a statutory duty. The best they could come up with was a cut in the grant to the Everyman Theatre (at £3,000, a relative fleabite, compared to overall spending) and discontinuing a gramophone record initiative by the library service. The prospective Conservative candidate for Reading, Peter Emery, described it rather ungrammatically as 'a sign of the biggest piece of bureaucratic mismanagement by a socialist council as I have come across'. There were no similar complaints in the press when, later in the year, it was announced that the budget for the royal visit had been overspent by 52 per cent.

Another council initiative came to final fruition. A mere three and a half years after it had been submitted to the Ministry of Housing and Local Government, the Development Plan for Reading received Government approval. Their long and detailed scrutiny had apparently left it virtually unchanged, including the long-term plans to create a new civic centre opposite the university site on the London Road. The paper was scathing about the prolonged history of the search for a new civic centre, which could be traced back to the first years of the century:

> Half a dozen sites have been explored, each further removed than its predecessor from the realities of a workaday world, till the peak of impossibility was reached with a grandiose scheme for an island site west of St Mary's Butts.
> The *Chronicle* said at the time that nothing would come of it. Nothing did.

The Ideal Homes Exhibition had home automation as its theme. Among the wonders brought to an expectant nation were Britain's first spin dryer, an electric food mixer, a bed warmer, aluminium foil for cooking and cream cheese in tubes.

Race relations in Reading suffered a setback when the paper accepted an advertisement for factory workers which specified 'no coloureds'. Two people wrote to complain about this to the paper and another wrote to the firm, saying that they were going to boycott its products in future. When the paper followed it up, the firm told them that there had been an error, that the wording should have read 'no **objection to** coloureds', and that their premises were a model of multi-racial harmony. How strange that, despite being alerted to the mistake, they had made no effort to correct this gross slur on their shining employment practices until the paper got in touch with them?

Top of the class in getting it completely wrong was this confident prediction in an advertisement feature from a local television supplier:

Colour television is the 'biggest and most expensive flop in the world' according to Mr B.C. Flemming-Williams, who is in charge of the colour television laboratories at Enfield. He predicted that CBS and Dumont, two of the three United States companies transmitting colour, will cease to do so soon and the third, RCA, will follow. This makes pretty authoritative confirmation of the summing up of the situation I gave you six months ago.

There are several reasons why colour is a dead loss. Firstly, the sets are too complicated, each of them having at least 42 knobs – any one of which can make the picture worse. Secondly, the cost; even a tube for a colour set costing one and a quarter times as much as a complete black and white set. Thirdly, manufacturers and advertisers are backing out because the colours do not do justice to their products.

The Roads Campaign Council visited Reading, calling for more spending on roads. They said that 'if nothing more were done in the near future than had been done over the last ten years, traffic on our roads might well come to a standstill'. Their main requirement was for a trunk road from London to the west of England, running to the south of Reading. It had first been proposed in 1946 and would relieve Reading of much of its through traffic. All that was missing was the name – the M4.

Somebody who clearly needed wider roads, at the very least, was the deputy coroner for Berkshire, who went on what sounds like a one-man attempt to drum up trade for his profession. He was fined £70 for reckless driving, after his car knocked two cyclists off their bikes, mounted the pavement and demolished a lamp-post. The police were particularly struck by the almost total absence of brakes on his vehicle, but he explained that his practice was to use the gears to slow down.

If the coroner did not have a leg to stand on, one of the cases to come up before his court had an even more serious shortage in the nether limbs department. Youth club organiser Jeffrey Marshall had been playing the part of Long John Silver in *Treasure Island* and, for reasons about which the court could only speculate, tried to drive home with his leg still strapped up behind him. It will not come as a total surprise that he drove into the back of a lorry, tragically with fatal results.

Reading Football Club was in dire straits. They had an overdraft of £23,000 and losses of almost £7,000 accumulated over the past year. They owed money to everyone – to other teams who had transferred players to them, to the bus company who provided their coaches, even to the laundry that washed their kit. The mayor launched a £10,000 trust fund appeal to bail them out of their immediate problems. In the very same week that local people were wondering if the team were worth investing in, they duly went down to their heaviest defeat since the war – 8–3 to Brighton. By the following week, the mayor reported that the fund had not received a single penny in contributions and, by June, lack of response and rows between the trustees led to calls for the appeal to be closed. But by the summer, the fund boasted the magnificent sum of £235 (plus another £1,500, promised by local industry if the balance could be raised by the general public).Of this sum, £200 had been promised by the local papers and a further

£25 from the licenced victuallers, making the general public's contribution around £10.

At their annual general meeting, the club's shareholders voted unanimously to scrap the trust fund plans. The club's accounts for the season 1956/57 showed that it was the Entertainments Tax that had turned a modest profit into a loss of £6,910. The abolition of that tax led the paper to hope that the club's finances had turned the corner. One sign of the times was that their income figures made no mention of earnings from merchandising replica kit or other products. The supporters launched their own appeal fund, which boosted the initial £235 up to the giddy heights of £300 by late August.

By November, the supporters had raised the first £500 for the club, which was handed over at a cup tie at Elm Park against Swindon, attended by some 21,000 supporters. This figure was more than the entire population of Wisbech, a tiny non-league club against whom Reading were drawn in the next round, and whom they only just managed to beat.

Someone who seemed to be making rather more money out of football than Reading Football Club was ex-amateur Reading player Ron Barrett of Tilehurst. He won 'a fortune' on Littlewoods Pools and told the reporter he was in a daze, wondering what to do with it. He thought he might give up work and open a sporting goods shop, and buy a new house, but still within walking distance of his beloved Elm Park. His fortune amounted to £45,529.

One famous figure from Reading's past who allegedly made a reappearance in 1957 was King Henry I. Ever since he was first buried in Reading Abbey in 1135, people had claimed to have dug him and his solid silver coffin up at regular intervals. But this time, science was on the case. A diviner claimed to have discovered the whereabouts of the coffin, using a bizarre-looking American-designed electronic gadget. Major C.A. Pogson of Hove learned his trade divining for water in the Indian Army between the wars, but had now expanded his activities to encompass oil, gas and, it appears, silver coffins. He was doing a tour of archaeological sites, looking for precious finds. Unfortunately for him, it was not just a question of taking out a spade and testing his theory. Government permission was needed to excavate this ancient monument.

Two pieces of historic Reading were about to disappear. The Abbey Mills were to cease production, some 800 years after the monks of Reading Abbey first harnessed the waters of the Holy Brook to produce flour. They had been in the same family – the Soundys – for over a century. Today, only an arch over the Holy Brook survives from the original medieval mill.

In Hosier Street, where the market now stands, Finch's Buildings were threatened with redevelopment to provide a school playground. By this time run down and subdivided, they were none the less some of the oldest surviving buildings in Reading. Stones from Reading Abbey had been used to build them, and they had once been the home of Lady Vachell and her husband, John Hampden. One of the leaders of the parliamentary cause against King Charles I, Hampden was at one time the most popular man in England, and his attempted arrest by the king was one of the factors that provoked the Civil War. It was said that Lady Vachell watched the progress of the parliamentary siege of Reading from the roof of the house, and her husband was to meet his

Finch's Buildings, a little part of Reading's history. The former stately home was divided into cottages in the eighteenth century.

death on the battlefield at Chalgrove Field. Their home survived them by some three hundred years.

There were signs of a changing climate of opinion in relation to smoking, though not on the part of the editorial column:

> Birmingham City Council has refused to forbid smoking on buses. If the same question arises here, we trust Reading will show equal wisdom. The policy of the government over the vexed question of tobacco and lung cancer, as is stated in the House of Commons, is to move by exhortation and not compulsion. To forbid smoking in public places is defended under the far-fetched pretext that a ban on his or her elders is a form of exhortation to the young idea. Actually it is nothing else than bringing in compulsion by the back door. Surely the sensible thing is to face up to the reality that, whatever authority may say, smoking will go on in some form and to concentrate upon eliminating the alleged deleterious substances in tobacco which are considered to be the cause of the trouble.

Rag Day 1957, and a Sputnik hovers over Station Road.

On the Women's Page, Redina quoted the view of the Tobacco Manufacturers' Standing Committee, that the case for cigarettes causing lung cancer was not proven. Her view was that cigarette craving was caused by low blood sugar levels, and that the cure was to suck a glucose tablet whenever you felt like a smoke.

The space age arrived with the launch of the first Sputnik. The main impact of this in the local paper was to heat up the debate about Civil Defence. Some felt this advance in technology simply underlined the futility of trying to protect the civilian population against the bomb. The local Trades Council withdrew its support for Civil Defence on this basis, declaring it to be a complete waste of time and money. Supporters argued that this was being 'defeatist' and that some protection was better than none. The Chairman of the County Civil Defence Committee said that World War Three with Russia was 'practically inevitable'. We should all go on whitewashing our windows, just in case. . . .

Christmas was coming, and what were the people of Reading buying in 1957? For little girls, there was the new Palitoy doll at 49s. 'She's almost human', claimed the advertisements, 'she blows bubbles, drinks from a bottle, says "Mama" and is indestructable.' Yes, that's almost human all right – sounds like most of my friends. The boys might go for Super Soccer, the magnetic football game that was 'brimming over with excitement that brings all the thrills of soccer into the home' – and all for just 35s. Mum could have a handbag – 12s 11d for the plastic variety, or £5 19s 11d for one in lizard skin, in the days before lizards had civil rights. And dad might like a Brownie 127 camera

THE BOMB

Don't be an Ostrich

Take a look. You can help

IN AN H-BOMB WAR, more lives would be in danger—more lives that could be saved only by a trained civil defence. Skill—the skill to cope with emergencies — is what will save lives and relieve suffering. It's not enough to be willing when the time comes. You'll be twice as useful if you *know* what to do.

ENROL AT:—TOWN HALL; HEADQUARTERS, DUKE STREET; LIBRARIES; POLICE STATIONS; W.V.S., LONDON STREET

Now more than ever we need

TRAINED CIVIL DEFENCE

There was much argument over the value of Civil Defence.

gift outfit, which for 35s 9d gave him a camera, case, neck cord and two films (but no flash). Anyone requiring a good laugh at Christmas could not go wrong with a tie clip in an amusing design (from 3s 6d) or a novelty tea towel for 3s 11d. I still don't know what the novelty was – perhaps they caught fire when they came into contact with water? For those on whom you did not wish to spend too much, Boots' gift vouchers could be had from as little as 1s and even Wrigley's chewing gum advertised itself as the ideal stocking filler.

Those with more money could have a combined radiogram and cocktail cabinet for 65 guineas. But if you wanted something really prestigious to keep your drinks in, and were not too bothered about how they might affect the sound, a Steinway grand piano could be yours for just 285 guineas.

NINE

1958: Banning the Bomb, and the Smoke

Just before Christmas, there was an explosion at the Atomic Weapons Research Establishment at Aldermaston, in which a worker was killed. The usual questions were asked about safety at the plant, but we knew that all was well when, in the New Year's Honours List, no fewer than five of the managers of AWRE received honours. These included a knighthood for William Richard Joseph Cook, the Deputy Director.

A more immediate threat to your health was breathing. A gruesome exhibition at Reading Library by the National Smoke Abatement Society showed how much gunge was contained in 70 cubic feet of air (the amount you would inhale in four hours). Among the educational exhibits was a comparison between a country-dweller's pink lungs and the grey ones of a townie. Just in time, it seemed, the final provisions of the Clean Air Act 1956 came into effect. A Smoke Control Scheme for Reading was one of a number submitted for approval to the Minister. Under this, 106 acres in the Coley Park area became a Smoke Control Area, a pilot to show what could be achieved elsewhere in the town.

A rising star was recruited to judge the Miss Reading 1958 competition held at the St Valentine's Ball in Reading town hall:

> Who is Benny Hill? He started life as a milkman, but a few years ago his talent for comedy was discovered and he has rocketed to the top of his profession. Last year he headed the bill at the Prince of Wales Theatre, London. Last weekend on BBC Television he scored another success with the first of a new series of 'The Benny Hill Show'. His debut in Reading promises one thing – a Red Letter Day for his fans and an enlightening one for those who do not yet know Benny Hill. His brilliant skits and ideas of fun are some of the brightest and best on television today.

One of Miss Reading's first duties was an unscheduled one. She was 'kidnapped' by Reading University students during Rag Week and 'held to ransom' for £5.

Benny Hill presents Miss Reading with her prize.

Miss Reading samples the latest product of Reading's aviation industry, at Woodley Aerodrome.

The cost of broadcasting programmes like Benny Hill was revealed in the *BBC Handbook*, published early in the year. Television broadcasts were now averaging £3,256 an hour (up from just £2,675 the previous year), while radio was relatively cheap at £575 an hour (up from £540). There were still at this time some 16 million households nationwide with a radio, but no television, though most Reading households were now viewers – the town had some 26,777 television licence holders by 1958 (and no doubt others, who had 'overlooked' the need to buy a licence).

One place where the television was not popular was in pubs. Licencees who tried it complained that the customers were so glued to it that they bought less beer, while the customers said that it was difficult to watch because of all the coming and going, not to mention the chattering of those anti-social people who went to the pub for conversation, rather than to watch the box.

But the cinema was suffering badly from the competition. During the year, the Gaumont on Broad Street closed, to be replaced by a branch of Timothy Whites (where Boots now stands). The Rex Cinema on Oxford Road closed, and there were rumours that the Savoy on Basingstoke Road was threatened with conversion into a shop. Also lost was the Regal in Caversham. Planning applications to use these latter premises for industrial purposes were refused, and the letting agents thought they might make a good dance-hall. In the end, after an interminable planning battle, the site became part of the Waitrose supermarket development.

In fact, landmarks were coming under threat with alarming regularity, as the development boom began to get under way. In the same week that Finch's Buildings were finally agreed for clearance, the vicarages of both St Mary's and Greyfriars churches came up for redevelopment. Plans to demolish the listed St Mary's Vicarage and replace it with an office block were refused by the council, though they accepted the principle of using the existing buildings

'I say, Penelope. Let's go and dig those crazy Kats!' Did people really talk like that?

for offices. The council also gave its blessing to the replacement of Greyfriars Vicarage with shops and offices. Their main motivation appeared to be the need to widen the road at that point to ease the flow of traffic. The only remaining obstacle was the small matter of ministerial approval. As we will see, this story was to rumble on into 1959.

Later in the same year, St Giles' Buildings in Southampton Street, opposite St Giles' Church, were approved for demolition. Built in about 1723 as a workhouse, that use ceased when the Central Workhouse came into being in 1835. In recent years the buildings had been vacated and had been allowed to fall into disrepair. The Shades public house on Gun Street also closed, earmarked for demolition to provide a 'Broad Street by-pass' linking Queens Road with Gun Street. Built in about 1600 and originally called The Dolphin, it had been closely linked with the Oracle workhouse, which stood next door. Until 1816 there had been a lock-up attached to it, where the nightwatchmen would incarcerate anyone they arrested on their rounds, in the days before Reading had a proper police force. Happily, this was one landmark that has survived demolition to this day.

Developers were active everywhere. Members of the Eye and Dunsden Parish Council were up in arms at proposals to extract 180 acres of gravel-bearing land at Dean's Farm in Caversham, leaving behind a large lagoon. Quite apart from the disturbance of fifty lorries trundling in and out every day and the effects on the natural beauty of the area, they were worried that a large area of stagnant water would become a breeding ground for mosquitos.

Reading Borough Council had no shortage of other arguments over the course of the year. The row about the site of the new Civic Centre was still going on.

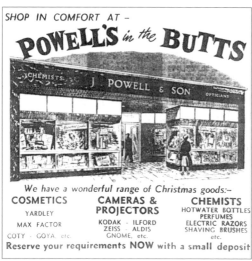

Lost retailers of the 1950s.

The plans to build it at London Road were scrapped in favour of 'somewhere more central' (precise location yet to be specified, though the Hosier Street area was again being mooted in the first half of the year), and the paper was scathing about the continuing delay and vacillation: 'Seldom in the town's story has a project been so badly bungled.' The paper was particularly rude about plans to include a civic theatre in the final stage of the scheme:

> No one regrets more than we do that fashion in Reading as elsewhere has set against the living theatre. But the unhappy fact remains. In this age of television, those who cling to the 'legitimate' grow daily fewer. By the time the Civic Centre is built, if it is ever built, how many will be left?

But the ambitions of Reading Borough Council as impresario appeared to know no bounds. In addition to the Civic Theatre proposals and their sponsorship of the Everyman Theatre, they even attempted to take over the lease of the Palace Theatre.

Also in dispute was the mayor's transport. One party wanted to buy him a chauffeur-driven car of his own, while the other favoured renting, at a saving of at least £1,000 a year. In a reversal of the positions taken many years later, it was Labour who were calling for the expensive option and the Conservatives who wanted to save money. At the same time, all the council's budgets were being referred back to their respective committees, to see if further savings could be made to keep the rates down.

One trip for which it seemed the mayor would not need a car was the one to the opening of the new Alice Jenkins Home for the Elderly. The council decided (again controversially) to break with tradition and invite the local MP, rather than the mayor, to perform the ceremony. Alice Jenkins, who had been the town's mayor herself in 1936, was a lifelong socialist, and it was felt that Ian Mikardo's politics would have been more to her taste than those of the current mayor. In the event, the mayor had the last laugh – Ian Mikardo was ill in hospital at the time of the opening and the mayor had to do the honours.

Tenants of the new multi-storey flats along the Bath Road were unhappy about their heating. They were paying 10s 10d a week for a heating system that was turned off between May and October. Even when it was on, it only built up a reasonable level of heat at the weekends. For the rest of the time, the tenants

Here's a man who knows the way to a woman's heart!

had to wrap themselves in dressing gowns or rugs to keep warm. The tenants also missed the cosy glow of a coal fire. They wanted out of the scheme, or at least to be given control of it by individual metering. A council spokesman explained, without winning many converts among the tenants: (a) that the cost was averaged out across the year and that the real running cost in the winter months was more like 21s a week; (b) that the new flats were still drying out and (c) that the electric underfloor heating was only ever intended to provide background heating, and that tenants needed to use other heaters (or a dressing gown or rug?) if they wanted extra warmth.

There were even fears among grave owners (as opposed to occupiers, presumably) in the old Reading Cemetery that the Borough Council had plans to turn the area into a pleasure garden. A public inquiry had to be held to hear their objections. The council was at pains to emphasise that this was not their intention. They were looking to acquire the cemetery from the private owners, who were in some difficulty maintaining it, and a legal loophole of some kind meant that the council did not have powers to acquire it as a cemetery, but could buy a pleasure garden. They promised it would remain a cemetery for as far as could be seen into the future.

Reading Borough Council were not the only ones seeking new premises. Berkshire County Council were at this time scattered around various premises in Reading town centre, known to the staff by such endearments as 'the cowshed' and 'the pigsty'. There were plans to construct a new building to bring them all together, involving a cost of over £400,000 and a building time of four years. They could go either on a site between the Abbey Ruins and Kings Road, near the old Shire Hall in the town centre, or out at a site they owned at Maiden Erlegh. The paper was in no doubt which one they should choose:

It is true that a County Council need not necessarily have their headquarters in a town, but, where they do not, all concerned and especially the general public must be put to a great inconvenience. From the particulars given in the joint committee's report it would appear that all the accommodation needed for many years to come can be obtained in a stone's throw of Shire Hall, and the difference in cost is not sufficient to cause concern.

News of the Munich Air Disaster came in during February. It had special significance for Reading, since the injured Manchester United manager Matt Busby had been a 'guest' player for Reading throughout the war years. One of those killed, former England and Manchester City goalkeeper Frank Swift, had also played for Reading while stationed close by.

High fashion, 1950s style.

There were calls for the Premium Bonds to have a weekly, rather than a monthly, draw, like the football pools. The idea came from Sir John Wolfenden, the Vice-Chancellor of Reading University. One problem was that it took ERNIE, the poor old primitive computer that generated the winning numbers, at least a full week to think up the numbers of the 6–7,000 winners of the monthly draw.

A number of important developments took place on the transport front. A Committee of Inquiry into the Inland Waterways of Great Britain decided that there was no case for reopening the Kennet & Avon Canal for commercial traffic – any restoration should be purely for its amenity and recreational value. Reading Transport was in crisis, as its finances dropped further into the red. Fare increases, designed to generate £63,000 extra income, were approved, and there were cuts in services (especially off-peak) which upset many. Apparently, one of the groups worst affected were those workers who still went home during their lunch hour, more of which was now spent waiting at the bus stop. Transport unions were also unhappy at their members' more limited chances to earn overtime. A committee of inquiry was set up to consider the future of Reading's public transport, and the usual calls were made to switch from trolleybuses to diesel power.

Plans were announced for what was referred to as 'The London–South Wales Motor Road' at Shire Hall. A proposed route for the section as far west as Reading was published. Not all the county councillors were in favour of the idea. One, who had seen the impact of a similar proposal between London and the north of England, described it as 'an appalling mess, doing far more damage than an atom bomb'. He went on: 'A more unfortunate thing to happen to the countryside cannot be imagined. I hope that, long before the London–South Wales Motor Road becomes final, the council will have a chance to try and minimise the damage it may cause.' There was more time than he thought. Later in the year, the government withheld funding for further development work on the plans.

Meanwhile, there were new ways of heading west from Reading:

WESTERN'S DIESEL SPEEDS TO BRISTOL
NEW STYLE LOCOMOTIVE SHOWS ITS PACES
A London-bound express thundered through Reading General station shortly before 11.30 a.m. on Monday, all impatient steamy arrogance. Out of its lingering spume there emerged, drawing solidly into Reading, an olive-green monster resembling the chopped-off head of a streamlined caterpillar, a faint shimmer of heat as it drew its nine coaches on what was a very historic occasion indeed.

For this 'caterpillar' was the locomotive *Active* (D600), the first of 130 diesel hydraulic locomotives ordered by British Railways for the Western Region, making a demonstration run from Paddington to Bristol and back. It pointed to the closure, comparatively soon, of the long and honourable reign of the steam engine; the familiar 'puff-puff' is on the way out; the 'rumbler' is taking over.

On Monday, the 2000 horse power *Active*, lugging 327 tons and its big complement of officials and guests, cut the normal running time from Paddington to Reading by well over five minutes despite a hold-up, and then, getting up speed between Wootton Basset and Chippenham until the indicator needle flicked over the 94mph mark, got

The first diesel express service passes through Reading.

to the Stapleton Road, Bristol station only slightly late of schedule – the full trip taking just over two hours.

That over-90 spell was more than a little exciting, a matter of national pride (there were foreign visitors on board). But it could hardly be described as comfortable. Coffee sloshed madly over the tables. Stewards lurched about despairingly, any idea of serving lunch having to be postponed until speed was reduced.

There were no such problems on the way back. One of the locomotive's two engines obligingly broke down, allowing the return journey to be covered at a sedate (and comfortable) 60mph.

Passing through Reading at an even more sedate pace was the march of the anti-nuclear demonstrators from London to Aldermaston. This took place over the Easter weekend, the demonstrators spending the third night of the march in Reading, before completing their journey to an Atomic Weapons Establishment that was closed for the holiday. The organisers expected anything up to a thousand marchers, accompanied by skiffle groups, jazz bands (including that of Humphrey Lyttelton) and a film crew under the control of Lindsay Anderson, recording the event for posterity. The editorial column was predictably scathing about the event:

> Those who think the world is going to be saved by 'a moral gesture' of this nature are deceiving themselves, as their fathers or elder brothers deceived themselves in

the 1930s. This kind of agitation in Britain and France then persuaded Hitler that the west was degenerate and he could with safety launch a war.

Conservatives on the council were equally opposed. References were made in the Council Chamber to the march being 'a political manoeuvre' and the marchers 'a motley collection' of 'wretched people'. Labour responded by declaring that the marchers were legally temporarily homeless and that it was the council's statutory duty to rehouse them overnight, in school premises.

Not everybody in Reading shared the dim view held by the local press. The writer J.B. Priestley drew a large crowd to Reading Town Hall, prior to the march, for a nuclear disarmament rally. (A collection held at the meeting raised the grand sum of £63 10s – and a button!) One fascinating fact to emerge from all the press coverage was that the distinctive symbol of the CND was based upon the semaphore signals for N (as in Nuclear) and D (for Disarmament).

The weather for the march that Easter was snowy and freezing. Some 1,200 marchers were welcomed in Reading town hall by Ian Mikardo. The only awkward moment came when a collection was taken and someone tried to divert half of the £115 proceeds into Labour Party coffers. After a protest, it was all given to CND.

CND marchers make their way along Castle Street, en route to Aldermaston.

What of the sporting events of the year? Reading Football Club almost won promotion out of Division Three but, after a 4–0 defeat by Swindon appeared to have cost them the championship, supporters attempted to present the club with a wreath. The club unsportingly declined to accept delivery. After narrowly missing out on promotion in 1957/58, the club started 1958/59 with high hopes. The club's finances were in better shape, thanks to the abolition of the Entertainments Tax and the supporters' rather more successful fundraising efforts. They bought three new players in the close season and were on the look out for more. Early in the season they led the league, having acquired 17 points in six weeks (and this in the days when a win counted for two points, not three). But, by Christmas, they had slipped back to fifth place.

Mixing in altogether higher footballing circles was twelve-year-old Terry Tilly of Pitcroft Avenue, who won the prize of a weekend with Stanley Matthews in a competition with the Co-op (retailers of Stanley Matthews' boots). Terry trained with the maestro and had dinner with him at a plush Blackpool Hotel, during which Stanley explained football tactics with the aid of a cruet set.

Sonning policeman Stan Eldon (later known locally for his involvement in the organising of the Reading Half Marathon) won the Berkshire AAA's 3-mile

PC Stan Eldon is filmed on his daily round by the BBC.

race in the second fastest time in the world seen that year. The time was set in waterlogged conditions at Palmer Park, in a race where he lapped all the other competitors. Had he had some competition, and had conditions been better, he might have gained a place in the record books. Having thus warmed up, he also entered and won the mile race at the same meeting *and* presented the prizes at the end. Later that year, the BBC TV programme *Sportsnight* made a film of him on his beat in Sonning. Heaven help any criminal who tried to do a runner in that village.

But the prize for sporting endeavour must surely go the the Trinity Cricket Club who, playing against Shinfield, managed to amass the grand total of 2 all out. Both runs were scored by their opening batsman (whose name was not preserved for posterity by the paper), though even he was dropped on 1, when the sun got in the fielder's eyes. The entire innings lasted 26 balls. Shinfield had previously scored 128 on a pitch described as 'lively'. Trinity's performance even eclipsed that of Shinfield's opponents the previous week, University Employees, who had set their opponents the daunting target of 5.

Bradfield College deserves a mention for an inspired piece of emergency planning. In order to add realism to their fire drill, someone set fire to a bucket full of wet brown paper. A total of eleven pupils ended up in the sanatorium, suffering from the effects of smoke inhalation.

From one form of environmental pollution to another – in what seems like a dress rehearsal for Reading Rock Festivals of future years, a skiffle contest at Caversham Court, organised by the YMCA, led to complaints from residents of the Warren about the noise. Attempts to turn the amplifiers down were apparently cancelled out by extra fervour on the part of the performers. The noise problem was not helped by the fact that the result of the competition was judged on the volume of the applause for each act. For the record, the competition was won by the Gordon Taylor Skiffle Group. But special mention must go to the L Seven Group from Reading Grammar School, who took second place despite two broken guitar strings and 'a minor derangement of the washboard'. As Master of Ceremonies Don Park said: 'Where else could you get such a good show for two bob?' (or for free, if you were an ungrateful resident of the Warren)?

Local newspaper readers were following a lurid case of attempted murder, where a man from Beverley Road in Tilehurst tried to drown his wife in the bath. It appears that theirs had been a happy marriage until he suffered a mental breakdown, the product of excessive study in an effort to 'improve himself'. Having committed the deed, the man ran naked into the garden where, after trying to steal a neighbour's baby from a pram, he knelt on the lawn, crying 'Christ is risen!' and waving his arms about. Neighbours rushed into the house and tried to resuscitate the wife, whereupon he attacked them with a carving knife. When the police arrived, he refused initially to get dressed, on the grounds that 'they don't wear clothes in hell'. Happily, his wife recovered in hospital. Questioned about the event, he said 'I cannot think what came over me.' The courts also recognised that he had not been himself that day. More serious charges were dropped and he was sentenced to a year's probation for grievous bodily harm, on condition that he spent a similar period in a mental hospital.

Brother Mandus, at St Lawrence's Church, calls on the faithful to rise up and walk.

Perhaps Brother Mandus could have helped him. He was a faith healer on a worldwide healing crusade, who drew a crowd of 700 to St Lawrence's Church. Forty of the congregation afterwards claimed cures for illnesses as diverse as asthma, arthritis, blindness and heart conditions.

Christmas approached, and the Roman Catholic Knights of Columba called for Reading retailers to put the Christ back into Christmas by using Christian imagery such as the crib in their window displays. Their campaign did not have a marked impact on the usual orgy of spending, but anyone who still had 7s 6d left over after the festive season could buy a seat at a Palace Theatre show in the new year. On the bill was a young man who was himself to become a famous Christian icon although he had not yet discovered his vocation. His backing group still called itself the Drifters and he had not long since ceased to be known as Harold Webb. It would be some years before he would be *Sir* Cliff Richard.

Ten

1959: Minis and Mikardo

The Christmas and New Year festivities in Berkshire were marred by a spate of accidents on the roads. A total of seventy-four serious accidents were reported over the festive season and, on Christmas Eve alone, twenty-six people were injured and three killed.

The newly formed Berkshire Child Guidance Clinic reported to the Education Committee on the growth of a disturbing new phenomenon. They were finding that an increasing number of children were being referred to them with a fear of school, sometimes amounting to panic. They christened the phenomenon 'school phobia'. It occurred mostly around the transition period between primary and secondary school and generally appeared to affect only well-behaved, sensitive, shy children of good intelligence (so I must have had something different). The problem, they concluded, lay with the mothers:

> In the home there is one striking feature which is present in varying degree. The mother is in some way emotionally dependent upon having the child close to her. She may be aware of this, openly declaring that she cannot stand being alone, or she may not be fully aware of it. The result is that, despite her conscientious efforts, she is unable to make a really whole-hearted effort to get the child to school.

Prosecution apparently only made the problem worse, and the only cure for some of the worst cases was treatment in an institution (for the mothers, that is). What effect this all had on the children and their attitude to school was not disclosed.

It was reported that 1958 had been a record year for rehousing Reading families. In the course of the year, a total of 841 families were rehoused, 593 of them moving into new homes. But, as Alderman Baker, Chairman of the Housing Committee, warned, the problem was growing almost as fast as they solved it. There were something like five hundred marriages in Reading each year and two years' residential qualification gave many couples almost enough points to get priority on the waiting list. For the Conservatives, Cllr Woodrow welcomed the achievement, saying that 'it is a matter completely outside politics'.

But politics got in the way of one major initiative by the council to solve its housing problems. They were close to striking a deal to purchase 137 acres of land at Caversham Park to build overspill council housing. (The area was at that time still outside the borough.) A price of £45,000 had been agreed as a basis for compulsory purchase. But the government then passed a law, saying that local authorities had to pay market price for any housing land it acquired. This immediately pushed the price up to £500,000 – way beyond what the council, or, more important, the eventual tenants of the houses, could afford. So it was that Caversham Park Village became a private, rather than a council, estate.

In the courts, the evil influence of television revealed itself in an unexpected way. Police spotted a van with a queue of traffic behind it. It was weaving about, preventing the cars behind from overtaking and threatening the oncoming traffic. When stopped, the driver explained that he had been singing a television jingle about 'happy motoring' to himself and moving his body about as he did so, causing the car to swerve. But something in this perfectly reasonable story did not add up to the eagle-eyed arresting officer. Possibly it was the fact that the driver's speech was slurred, that his eyes could not focus, that he could not walk down a straight line without falling over or remember his registration number without looking at it. Possibly it might even have been the fact that he smelt strongly of alcohol. In any event, the man was convicted of drunken driving.

A well-known landmark at the end of West Street was under threat of redevelopment. Greyfriars Vicarage was attributed to the locally born, but nationally famous, architect Sir John Soane (whose other works include the

What the well-dressed 1950s child and teenager were wearing.

Bank of England in the City of London and the monument to Reading Mayor Edward Simeon in Market Place). Redevelopment had been mooted since 1955 and the building had been listed as being of architectural and historic interest in 1957. Notwithstanding this, the council in 1958 gave its blessing to demolition and redevelopment, as we learned in the previous chapter. The matter was referred to the minister, leading to a public inquiry.

The prospective developers were the Church Council. They claimed that, whatever its architectural and historic interest, the building was entirely inconvenient and uneconomic and the only proper course was to redevelop it for shops and offices. Even the Bishop of Reading, the Rt Revd Eric Knell, appeared at the hearing to lend his weight to the developer's cause. The developer's counsel made this particularly touching case for demolition:

> This is obviously not a case where permission to develop is sought on a commercial basis. No one desires to make money out of it, although the site happens to be a valuable one. If permission to develop is given, the Church Council may decide to develop it for ecclesiastical purposes – for a church hall or something of the kind, and not in the form of shops and offices.

He also said that there were fairies at the bottom of his garden and that the moon was made of green cheese. (No, he didn't really, but it would have been no more implausible than any of the foregoing.) Happily, the inspector was not taken in by any of it and the vicarage remains at the end of West Street to this day.

On the subject of tasteful development, St Mary's Vicarage was sold for £20,000 to former Conservative Councillor W.A. Alexander. He announced plans to build a 20,000 square foot office block 'of dignity and beauty' on the cleared site – if he could just be allowed to knock down the existing listed building, in the interests of dignity and beauty.

Also under threat was Mapledurham Mill. The medieval mill had suffered fire damage in 1955 and needed at least £1,000 spent on it. It was felt unlikely that it would ever return to its original use. Henley Rural District Council was strongly opposed to its demolition, though the owners later denied that this was intended – at least, until all other possibilities had been exhausted.

The editorial column displayed its faith in the inexorable march of progress. People were lamenting the gradual passing of steam locomotives in favour of the diesel variety. The paper reminded them that, a century before, similar sentiments had no doubt been voiced about the replacement of horse power by steam. But more change was to be anticipated:

> Within a generation, as seems likely, the oil age will itself have passed as the new giant of nuclear power takes control. It is to Harwell and Calder Hall that British industry must look for its salvation.

Someone less captivated by the applications of nuclear energy was Labour councillor Miss Inez Randall. She had been detained at a demonstration at an atomic weapons base in Norfolk. When she failed to give an undertaking not to go near the base again, pending her trial, police arrived at her house and took her away to Holloway Prison in the full glare of the local media. After she had served her fourteen days, she gave the press a detailed account of the degrading prison regime, which gave no thought, as she put it, to 'the spiritual or moral uplift of the inmates'.

Somebody else whose dignity was under threat was the mayor. The row about the mayoral car was still rumbling on and one of the arguments put forward by the ruling group on the council was that 'the dignity and position of the mayor should be upheld in every respect', and that it was 'undignified for him to have a different car every year'. The rest of us should be so lucky.

The word 'dignity' hardly applies to some of the university students' Rag Week stunts. They decided to organise a campaign in favour of nuclear arms, in opposition to that of CND. Their tasteful campaign symbol was a triple mushroom cloud, and their 'march' led away from Aldermaston, into Reading. In another stunt, they adorned the statue of Edward VII outside Reading station with a full set of ladies' underwear, streamers and a placard saying 'Woops! I'm a fairy!' None of this excited any adverse comment in the press.

Another student stunt in rather better taste had the national newspapers and BBC TV rushing to Reading, to report the discovery of diamonds in the Thames Valley. A member of the academic staff was recruited to add credibility to the claims. When the spoof was discovered, *The Times* and others wrote pompous editorials, denouncing the wasting of the press's valuable time.

Rag Day procession and the students go ballistic. Note the lethal dual carriageway in Broad Street, with pedestrians forming the central reservation.

Aldermaston enjoyed some other unwelcome publicity during the year. An explosion at the Atomic Weapons Establishment early in the year killed two people and injured another. The authorities said no nuclear materials were involved – the accident occurred while they were dealing with conventional explosives. But local people got nervous – it was like living on the edge of a volcano, said one. The inquest could find no reason for the explosion, and recorded a verdict of accidental death. Questions were asked about it in Parliament.

Another incident in Aldermaston caused large-scale pollution of the Rivers Kennet and Thames. But for once it was not the fault of AWE. Floods ripped away part of the riverbank, rupturing a pipe and causing hundreds of gallons of petrol from a fuel depot at Aldermaston to spill into the river. The paper was able to report that thirty-four swans and fourteen ducks were affected by oil. River users were advised not to throw lighted cigarettes into the water.

Cliff Richard appeared at the Palace Theatre, but was inaudible throughout his performance, owing to the screaming of his fans. They also threw cakes at the stage (for reasons now lost in the mists of time). Attempts by the eighteen-year-old rock and roller to calm his admirers proved totally unsuccessful. At the end of the performance, about three hundred of them rushed outside to the stage door, ready to show their adoration by tearing him limb from limb the moment he set foot outside. When he unobligingly failed to offer himself up for sacrifice, some of them amused themselves by trying to turn over a passing car. What it is to be young and in love!

Cliff visits the Palace – but not to collect a knighthood this time.

But Reading's own pop idol was waiting in the wings. Eighteen-year-old Dean Webb (better known to his mother as Michael Eaton, of Thirlmere Avenue) had been signed up by the same man – John Foster – who had apparently started Cliff Richard on his career. Dean was linked with a record company, and was scheduled to appear on television's 'big beat musical spectacular' feature *Oh Boy!* Dean/Michael had begun his career as an apprentice blacksmith at the old smithy in Merchants' Place. He left there to seek fame on the stage with his band, 'The Blue Jeans Boys', in which he was known as Gerry Grant. His former employer said of Dean/Michael/Gerry, 'he would have been a good blacksmith'. Whether or not this was a comment on his musical skills we may never know, but he certainly looked the part. His picture in the paper had him striking the the kind of knock-kneed pose favoured by 1950s rock and roll artistes (and incontinence sufferers).

His chances of starring at the Palace Theatre were beginning to look thin. After the Borough Council's takeover plans came to nothing, it was closed temporarily during the year, giving rise to speculation about its future. One story was that its owners, the Rank Organisation, were about to convert it into a television theatre. However, the theatre continued to stage shows sporadically up to the end of the year. The Majestic Ballroom was definitely closing. This former Corn Exchange had been a roller-skating rink before the war, but had flourished as a dance hall under its present management for fourteen years.

More stars were in evidence, but this time in the open air, on Good Friday, when an All Stars XI football team took on Huntley & Palmers in a charity football match. The scoreline – 9–6 – suggests that the match was not played in an entirely serious vein. Tommy Steele was the All Stars' star, so to speak, with four goals. Also appearing for them were actor Alfie Bass, comedians Mike and Bernie Winters, Dave King, skiffler Lonnie Donegan and Jess Conrad, who was later to earn lasting fame by being voted the worst pop singer in the entire history of rock and roll.

The Aldermaston March this year attracted some 6,000 marchers, several times the expected number. They certainly registered their presence in Reading, contributing to major traffic jams. Shoppers trying to cross Broad Street were swept out towards Aldermaston.

Broad Street was apparently chaotic enough under normal circumstances. People complained that the bus stops there caused traffic chaos, and that the queues got so tangled up, it was sometimes impossible to know which one to join. The new one-man buses were said to make a bad situation worse. A local police superintendent had the answer – fence in the main pedestrian footpaths, allowing crossing only at a limited number of controlled points, ban on-street parking and build a whole host of bypasses, relief roads and motorways. It will come as no surprise to learn that he was speaking at the lunch of the Traders' Road Transport Association, and that there were no reports of rioting from his audience in protest against these suggestions.

There were more signs of change in the world of transport. Congestion in Reading generally was getting so bad that a host of new 'no waiting' streets were introduced, stretching from Wokingham Road in the east to Oxford Road in the west. Conservatives complained that the council was driving cars out of town and 'harassing the poor wretched motorist', and there were calls for a one-way system to sort out the town centre.

Britain had its first experience of motorways, as they now called them, with the opening of the M1 between London and Birmingham. Reading had a special interest in this, since the emergency breakdown service on it was run remotely from the AA's Reading offices. Some firms banned their lorries from using it, since they did not have brakes powerful enough to deal with motorway traffic speeds.

Late in the year, the car that came to epitomise the 1960s, the Mini, was born. With its rubber suspension, front wheel drive and transverse engine, it caused quite a stir and made some of its competitors look very old-fashioned. By comparison, about all that the 1959 Morris Minor could boast in the way of improvements was that the horn button was now situated in the middle of the steering wheel (as opposed to where? In the boot?).

The Mini appeared in 1959 and set new standards for small cars.

The war against a number of infectious diseases now regarded as things of the past was yet to be won. The last case of diphtheria in Reading was in 1948, but the health authorities were still on their guard against further outbreaks. That polio was an ever-present threat was brought home when footballer Jeff Hall, Birmingham City and England full back, died from the disease. He had lived and played near Reading during his National Service. Teams at Elm Park that weekend wore black armbands and held a minute's silence before the game. All Reading's players under twenty-five were made to have polio injections. (Were older members of the team considered to be expendable?)

Reading Football Club had other reasons for being in mourning. Their start to the 1959/60 season was the worst in years. By mid-September, they were at the bottom of the league, having gained only one point from a possible sixteen. After a more promising spell, the year ended with them only fourth from the bottom. During the autumn, they were thrashed 6–1 by West Ham in the Southern Cup and 5–2 by a Tottenham Hotspur team containing five internationals, in a testimonial for some of the long-standing Reading players.

Ice-cream, in the days before universal fridge ownership.

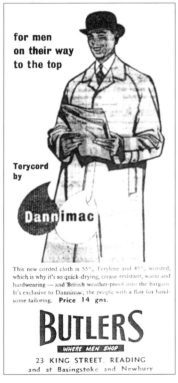

The 1960s fashion revolution was about to break, though you might not believe it from this advertisement.

To add to their pains, two of their Supporters' Club organisers were sent to prison for a series of frauds involving the Supporters' Club Football Pool. The only thing they had to look forward to as they entered the 1960s was a third round FA Cup tie against the cupholders, Nottingham Forest.

At least the ground had been improved, even if the team had not. The supporters' fundraising efforts had produced a total of £14,596 in two years, £7,737 of which had been spent on ground improvements. Somebody even suggested rather fancifully that the improved Elm Park, with its new tea stall, was now one of the best grounds in the country.

Nothing happened in Reading for much of the summer – or, if it did, posterity did not record it, since a printers' strike closed down the *Chronicle* for several weeks.

The Royal Berkshire Regiment was disappearing. They were merging with the Wiltshire Regiment to form the Duke of Edinburgh's Royal Regiment. In a dignified ceremony at Brock Barracks, their colours were trooped for the last time. This was in marked contrast to an event which took place shortly afterwards. Late one night, the neighbourhood around Brock Barracks was rocked by the sounds of a battle – involving thunderflashes, hosepipes and ancient muzzle-loading cannon filled with gunpowder, tennis balls and apples – in which the officers tried to 'capture' the sergeants' mess.

People living near the Barracks might be forgiven for wanting to get away from it all, and the papers early in the new year were increasingly offering that opportunity. Holidays in Europe could be had for as little as £14 14s, which was cheaper than the rail journey to most British resorts at the standard rate. Going abroad was starting to look very good value, compared with, say, eight days in Torquay for £19 2s or the massive £37 7s cost of a ten-day coach tour of Scotland.

News was announced of a further addition to the Duke of Edinburgh's own personal regiment, prompting this editorial comment:

THE QUEEN
The news of the forthcoming happy event in the Royal Family has given joy to Her Majesty's subjects in every part of the globe. In an age where long-accepted standards seem everywhere open to attack, the happy family life of the last two sovereigns has shone out like a beacon over a troubled sea.

Thus the *Chronicle* greeted the news of Prince Andrew's impending arrival. It would be a monarchist editor indeed that could write such an editorial in the mid-1990s.

The council had another ambitious capital project. Stung by criticisms of the town's inadequate swimming facilities, they came up with the idea of a massive Olympic standard pool with room for a thousand spectators. It would cost over £500,000 and was to be built on the Thameside Promenade, west of Caversham Bridge. This had the effect of uniting the ratepayers and the environmental lobbies in furious opposition. Eight hundred of them packed the town hall to voice their anger. The opposition led to the plans being scaled down later in the year and to alternative sites (such as Prospect Park or The

Dell, in London Road) being considered. However, the debate was far from being resolved as the 1950s ended.

Fourteen years as Reading's MP had not dampened Ian Mikardo's love of a good row. Among his causes of the year, he denounced the Street Offences Bill, designed to drive prostitution off the streets. All it would do, he said, was to sweep it under the carpet (which sounds a very uncomfortable place to conduct such business). Intriguingly, he told his audience that he had some knowledge of these matters, having experience of how New York call girls organised things. He was also accused of making disparaging remarks about his party colleague George Brown to Premier Khrushchev, during a visit to Russia. This he denied, saying that he was a victim of press distortion. He also described our own Prime Minister, Harold Macmillan, as the Americans' Archie Andrews (a well-known ventriloquist's dummy of the day – see chapter 1) for his policy on nuclear weapons. In short, a typical year.

It was, however, to be his last as Reading's MP. An election was called for 8 October and Mikardo's wafer-thin majority made his seat a prime target for the Conservatives. He faced a straight fight with a 33-year-old Conservative, Peter Emery. The Conservatives brought in heavyweight support, in the form of Minister of Labour Iain McLeod and Conservative Party Chairman Lord Hailsham. Hailsham, speaking to an audience consisting largely of Conservative ladies, made a particularly aggressive attack on Mikardo's extreme left-wing socialism. He described him as: 'the greatest asset to Conservative Central Office since Mr Bevan went out of business and Mr Michael Foot lost his seat in Parliament. Indeed, if I were being particularly Machiavellian, which is not in my character, I am not sure that I should not be secretly trying to get him in!' Mikardo accepted this singularly backhanded compliment in good part, saying: 'I think it is a great favour to be singled out by the leader of the Conservative Party'.

The campaign got predictably tetchy, with Emery accusing Mikardo of mudslinging, over claims by Mikardo that Emery had falsified advertised vacancies at a local factory for electoral purposes. Emery also took exception to Mikardo's appearance on a television programme during the campaign. The election produced a majority of 3,942 for the Conservatives, and everybody managed to be very nice to each other after the event. Even the editorial column managed to be moderately civil to Ian Mikardo for once:

> And so that doughty opponent, Mr Ian Mikardo, Labour's ambassador at large, whose monthly orations to his supporters in Minster Street have been entertaining even if they have been provocative, ceases to be a member.
>
> Since he successfully wooed the town there have been many times when the Berkshire Chronicle has crossed swords with him. More than once, he has acknowledged our fairness.
>
> It is a fitting tribute to the personality of one, who, whatever he has been, has never been dull, that this newspaper, through a decade and a half the most persistent critic of his politics, should echo in the hour of his defeat the once familiar words of a wartime song: 'We don't want to lose you, but we think you ought to go'.

Ian Mikardo campaigns outside Elm Park – but the supporters seem more interested in the game.

Do-it-yourself began to emerge as a popular pastime. There were initial fears that it would put tradesmen out of work, but in fact they probably made more money putting right some of the efforts of their amateur counterparts. Manufacturers began to supply materials and apparatus suited to amateur needs, though the day of the DIY warehouse had yet to dawn. The *Chronicle* launched a £200 competition to find the best DIY project. It drew a wide range of entries, from houses and boats, to a 10-foot astronomical telescope, a bird bath, a model village and, most curious of all, a portable brick garden wall.

Just before Christmas, news broke that a major biscuit manufacturer in the town was about to close, with the loss of between 250 and 300 jobs. It was not Huntley & Palmer but Serpells (whose centenary we celebrated in chapter 2). They blamed falling sales, rather than labour shortages, for the firm's demise.

So where was Father Christmas, you will all be asking? It depended on whom you believed. Wellsteeds claimed that he was with Aladdin in their Wonder Cave. The Co-op spread some rumours that he would be disembarking at Freebody's

A typical 1950s Christmas shopping scene.

landing stage by Caversham Bridge, from his cruiser. But the truth was that he was cruising around the town in a 1906 vintage Renault car, probably trying to pick up elves. We know this is true, because there was a picture of him in the paper.

And so the 1950s drew to a close. The paper's first editorial of the new decade took stock and waxed, if not lyrical, then certainly verbose, about the prospects for the future. In the days before the breakdown of the barriers between east and west Europe, before AIDS had been discovered and before the concern about man's ability to destroy his own environment by pollution had been clearly expressed, the big fear was the atomic bomb:

> By the time these words appear in print the stripling new year will have entered from the wings and made his bow.
>
> The old will have been ushered into the misty past to join ten thousand buried kings. What has the youthful ambassador in his Pandora's Box, and what has the patriarch left behind of value among the mixed wares he has vended among his brief sojourn?

The scroll of 1959 is now completely unrolled and from it the observant can estimate how far along the road of peace and security the nations are moving. Is there an inn in sight?

That international tension has been eased in the past year few would dispute, but there were periods of quiescence in the Hundred Years' War and Napoleon's aggression recoiled only to spring again.

The calm of this nuclear age is too near a calm despair, when poised over the countless millions a new monster has risen from the primeval slime to give pause to even the most ambitious seeker after world power. . . . As Winston Churchill once averred, what the future holds for the nation's happiness is limitless, if sanity and not folly can enter the hearts of men.

'The moth will singe her wings and singed return, her love of light quenching her fear of pain.' But man can make a choice.

In 1960 that choice will be before the statesman of the great powers, if they will but work in harmony for the common good. They bear a terrifying responsibility.